RERUN ERA

RERUN ERA

OR, THE DISLOCATIONS

JOANNA HOWARD

McSWEENEY'S
SAN FRANCISCO

McSWEENEY'S
SAN FRANCISCO

McSweeney's and colophon are registered trademarks of McSweeney's, an independent publisher based in San Francisco.

Printed in the United States.

ISBN: 978-1-944211-67-7

10 9 8 7 6 5 4 3 2 1

www.mcsweeneys.net

For my brother Donnie, remember remember

THERE ARE PICTURES OF DENNIS WEAVER AT MY FAVORITE ICE CREAM SHOP.

Joplin is forty minutes away, so it is an outing. Joplin is in another state. We go to another state for ice cream. We go to another state for everything. My dad works for a trucking company that is in another state, a third state, even. It's in between our state and this ice cream state, which doesn't even seem possible since everything is under an hour away. Under an hour.

And everything is flat and dry and a field or a long flat road. Everything is grass that is on its way out or on its way in. The seasons are the season of hot and muggy, the season of ice storms, the season of torna-dos. In the hot and muggy season we get ice cream most nights after my dad comes home from work.

I don't even really like ice cream as a kid. It is always being offered as a bribe for something, but then they get me the ice cream and I have to get another bribe to eat the ice cream. Ice cream is too controlling. There is a lot of guilting, guilting around the flavors, like when my mom's friend buys me German chocolate which is her favorite, a flavor that has coconut right in it. I scream. I scream bloody murder and drop down in the parking lot having a conniption. I hurl the ice cream at a parked car. I get half dragged away.

But in Joplin there is Anderson's where they have old-fashioned everything. This is not the time when old-fashioned things are thought to be good: this is a time when old-fashioned things are thought to be novelty and overpriced and dingy and generally for the elderly. When we go to the ice cream shop, it is always us and the elderly.

My dad doesn't mind the elderly. He gets along with everybody because of being from a place. When you are from a place forever, you know how to be with the people from the place even if you are younger. It doesn't matter that the place is in another state because all the states touch, so my dad gets to be from four of the states at once. We all do, but less so than my dad.

At Anderson's my dad gets black walnut every time. His honest favorite flavor of ice cream is black walnut, which to me tastes like mold and rot. We have a black walnut tree in our yard, where my little red swing is, and when the walnuts are ripe, I hop up and down in the swing and shake the limb, and the walnuts drop from the tree encased in their exterior balls of black ooze and they burst like bombs all over the lawn furnishings and walkways and stain everything a dark color. Black walnut, black walnut. My dad is obsessed. He panels the house in walnut, the hardwood floors are stained walnut. Walnut is a color of luxury.

But Anderson's has an old-fashioned vanilla ice cream cone that has been pre-dipped in the most lurid cherry-flavored wax and then frozen very solid. A row of these sit at the back of the freezer case waiting for me. As regards sweets, I like always the red things, and the pink things. I do not care for the chocolate things, or the butterscotch things or the things with nuts. If I am given a chocolate thing or a thing with nuts I scream and hurl it. But I enjoy the red and pink things. I think I can taste red and pink, and that is a flavor. (It is! It is fruit, this is not made up!) The man behind the counter wears a paper hat, and is a bit slow or slow of wits, and he looks both very old and very young, older than my parents in some ways, and young somehow too in his softness in his slow approach to the dipping of the homemade ice creams. Sometimes his father is there too, and he too seems both young and old at once. Perhaps it is the paper hat. The buzz cuts make their heads look like gray fuzzy baby heads. They have both always worked at the ice cream shop, my mom says, even since she was young, and they are part of a family bound by ice cream and paper hats, and also cinnamon rolls which cost five dollars. It is the paper hat father who is shaking hands with Dennis Weaver in the photographs on the wall.

I am docile. I have my red frozen thing. My mother points to the photographs.

That's Dennis Weaver, she says. I shrug. He's from Joplin, she says.

I shrug, I've heard it before.

He's so handsome, my mother says.

I guess, I guess he is, but I don't say. He has a mustache. I like mustaches. I came out of the womb liking mustaches, I don't know why.

He was Chester on Gunsmoke, my dad says, before Festus, he was Marshall Dillon's sidekick.

I like Festus, I say. I know my dad likes Chester better. I rebel. I rebel by preferring Festus.

I AM EASILY RATTLED.

My brother is so much older than me he is just: not—
he is not. Not there, not real, not known. Gone or
alone or elsewhere. He has a skateboard. He threat-
ens me with scissors if I knock on his door. When I
am very little he chases me in a Gene Simmons mask,
and scares me to death, and I run through the house
screeching. My mom explains it's not scary, it's just
a rock band that wears lots of white makeup and this
person has an especially long tongue. Like a demon?
And this is not scary? There is no logic to this.

I'm pretty easily rattled. I get scared if anyone
breathes like Darth Vader, for instance. (My brother

does it. He comes into my room and breathes like Darth Vader, and I scream and run through the house.) We go to the movies and my dad doesn't like to go because he is always working or fishing or in the woods, and my brother doesn't like to sit with my mom at the movies, so my mom takes me to the movies and has me sit with her for company and my brother goes elsewhere. We go to see Raiders. My brother has already seen it. Do not take her, my brother says, She's going to flip out at the end. I do fine for the whole film and then we get to the end, and they open the ark, and the faces melt and I flip out. I'm scared of Nazis after that. My mom says, Well, that's alright, Nazis are very scary. But also I'm scared of biblical artifacts?

My mom wants to see The Elephant Man and doesn't want to go alone. My brother says, Do not do this, do not take her to see The Elephant Man. My mom takes me. I am five. I scream, I wail, but my mom really wants to see the end of the movie so I have to sit there. To this day, I think I will die in my sleep if I lay flat, that my deformities will literally crush my lungs. I sleep with so many pillows; I sleep propped up, like a pneumonia patient.

EVERYTHING IS A RERUN.
OR A VARIETY.

It is us with the TV. We are all together there with the TV, and the TV is not somehow the same as the movies. Someone else is in charge of what goes on the TV besides my mom, so I will not see faces melting on the TV by accident. The TV is safe for now.

In the daytime there are reruns, and early in the day there are deep reruns, reruns from a truly bygone era. I can't connect to these reruns, they rely on a different humor and value system, such as the comedy of owning an icebox, or having a paper route. The value system I like is based more on soap operas and comic parodies of soap operas and films that are way over my head. I do it, sometimes. Yes, I watch Andy Griffith, I have to. There is nothing else on. But I do not understand about Davy Crockett. I simply do not. The theme song begins and I fly into a rage. I have to go outside. There is no choice. I have to go outside for at least an hour till it stops.

But then there is this golden twilight hour which is a transition period. A period where there are reruns of existing programs, reruns of the programs that are actually new and ongoing programs or programs at least with the potential for the new, the new and the old all at once! I can watch reruns in the day and then later, at night, watch new versions of the reruns. So I can watch M*A*S*H and it will be one with Trapper and Radar and Henry, and then an hour or so later, a new episode comes on with B.J. and Klinger and Colonel Potter. I have my preferences. I don't like B.J., I like Trapper. Trapper has curly blond hair and I think he is funnier. I think B.J.'s hair is a little bit thinning. Trapper and Hawkeye always wear their bathrobes, and Trapper's is blue. B.J. pretty much never wears a bathrobe. Plus I think he is married, and so there are no romantic antics. I enjoy the romantic antics. I don't mind Klinger, but I prefer Radar. He has a teddy bear and seems very competent. With M*A*S*H, I like the reruns best: everything gets serious after Henry dies. Everything gets very, very serious. I watch the episode where Hawkeye has dreams. It is the best and scariest episode ever of M*A*S*H, even though it is after Trapper, but then for a long time, I am scared to be drifting in a boat surrounded by prosthetic limbs. In that dream Hawkeye just drifts in a boat through a cove filled with plastic arms and legs, and then, he takes off his own arms and tosses them in and he is armless, in his fatigues, in his red bathrobe, which he always wears over his fatigues, like he's got a chill or something, but he's still on the job. Or like he is always in a state of sleeping or dreaming.

I want to be Hawkeye. I want to be from Crab-apple Cove and have a dad who reads *Last of the*

Mohicans while taking me out in our rowboat on the bay or inlet. My dad does not read so good, but he has a boat. I rarely go out in it, because it is a bass-pro type boat, that can go speedy or that can purr along at a good clip for trolling, and the last time I went out in it we were trolling and my favorite bunny went overboard and no one would go back for her. I began a tantrum. This went on for days. I don't go on the boat now except when it is parked in the driveway. I like the boat, it is red and sparkly and even the astro-turf carpeting is red. I like the rubber worms that go with the boat which are red and purple and jelly; they look edible. I try to eat them. Then I can only go on the boat in the driveway chaperoned.

It's hard to know how time works because of M*A*S*H, because of all the back and forth between the most present moments and the reruns. I forget which things are part of the narrative of the reruns and which things are part of the narrative of the current episodes. There is definitely a breakdown of linearity. And when is it set anyway? It is supposed to be the '50s perhaps, but at a certain point they just abandon the look of the '50s and everyone just looks like the '70s as if a war has been going for twenty-five years. It seems like it is about Vietnam, but it isn't. My mother likes me to understand about Vietnam, but I still don't understand about Vietnam. I definitely don't understand about Korea. Are these places or are these wars? First they are places. But for my mom they are only wars?

Why are there so many shows that are supposed to be the '50s but which look like the '70s? Why is this? There is the one with Andy and Opie, and the one with Fonzie, Potsie, and Chachi, and the one with Shirley, Lenny, and Squiggy. Everyone is just trying to get by in dreary cities like Milwaukee or Cincinnati in the '50s. People live in basements and over garages, and they will do almost anything for a buck, like working in breweries or waiting tables or trying to rig a dance contest. And their names are all diminutives of bigger names, like they are the namesakes of their own names. My brother and I are namesakes after my father, already, but Mom tacks an 'ie' on my name and on my brother's name. Everyone endures the eee-sound on their name until they can't anymore, until they are grown. That's how it works.

Everyone is always waiting for Taxi to come on. Everyone loves Taxi. Taxi is totally the now. Except my brother. My brother is elsewhere.

There are also the variety shows. We watch the more Western-based ones. The ones where sisters dress in matching chiffon ball gowns and do musical numbers and, presumably, comedic skits. Or where everything takes place in a cornfield, or on a hayride, and there are hillbillies and/or everyone makes fun of women's lib. My mom is a secretary and she subscribes to Ms. Magazine. She is unconvinced by the Western variety programs, possibly because of the short shorts or the implants or the way the women all seem dumb beyond imagination. I like them. Sometimes there is puppet crossover from kid-type variety shows, and the colors are lurid, outrageous, like in the funny papers.

My mom comes home early one afternoon and catches me watching Andy Griffith because I have absolutely no choice.

Your brother looked just like Opie when he was that age, my mom says. (Lie.) And he couldn't pronounce RFD, but he begged to watch it. (Doubtful.) My mom offers the mangled pronunciation of RFD as per her memory of my brother's youth tongue. This, I think, is exactly why he won't sit with you at the movies.

All my adventures are there, inside the TV.

I CUT MY KNEE
ON A MOUSETRAP.

Somehow, one day a mousetrap is wedged in the space between the cushion and the arm of my favorite TV-viewing armchair. My dad has been sitting in the chair that day sewing bacon onto the mousetraps and one trap has gone astray. He sews the bacon on because the mice are very delicate, very crafty, and if you just wedge the bacon on they will steal it without triggering the clapper arm which crushes them. We live on the edge of a field and so there are mice like crazy. There are so many traps scattered throughout the house, what seems like hundreds of traps. One must be aggressive, in such situations. There is one season when dad traps twenty-three mice in a week. He's very proud of his ability to trap and discard many field mice. Every time he gets one he comes through the room where I'm watching TV and dangles it between me and the TV. It's hard to come between me and the TV. We are at one.

I stick my knee down between the arm and the cushion, because why? Because I sort of kneel the whole time I am watching TV. And sometimes I spring or leap onto the back of something. The back of the armchair, or the back of a sofa. I imagine everything is a staircase that leads to an attic where there are old-timey things. I perch ready to climb up to the attic loft where our quilted counterpanes are laid out on our little beds, and there is a bath in a metal tub, and a pan of snow with caramel taffy cooling in it, and it is the attic of a tree, because at this time, I am interested in these books where well-dressed mice live in very fancy homes inside the trunks of trees, and the littlest mice dress in overalls and tea dresses and their rooms are at the very top of the tree, in the attic of the tree, and they are tucked into beds with fluffy, multicolored quilts. I am desperate to have an attic, but we live in a ranch-style. Everyone I know lives in a ranch-style. I have only one friend with stairs—she is my fanciest friend. She and her sister share rooms in what was once an attic, but which has been renovated with carpet and a small bathroom and Strawberry Shortcake wallpaper. It is my idea of paradise. I don't even know if I like the girl, I just want to go to her sleepovers because she has a stair and an attic. (Do you like our house? her mother asks me. I like it. Dennis Weaver's wife grew up in this house, she says. He's so handsome, I say. Yes, she says, and sighs.)

I perch in my chair, at one with the TV, ready to scale the arm of the chair toward the back of the sofa toward my imagined attic which is what: a space of air above the furniture, a space that leans against the wood paneling. The whole house is paneled. It sucks up light, even the light of the television. I perch, I crouch, I wedge my knee between the cushions and slice myself on the trap. My dad is pretty sorry for this later, he is pretty sorry for having left out a dangerous mouse-killing device in the space where I play.

WE ALL GO TO BRANSON.

Sometimes we take a vacation all together. To Silver Dollar City where they recreate pioneer days, and also Wild West days and gold rush days, and dust bowl days. They recreate all the difficult, dirty days. The City itself is made of dirty streets of straw and mulch, and black asphalt. People dressed as train engineers drive golf carts around on the mulch and asphalt parts. People dressed like pioneer ladies stir big kettles of lye soap and big kettles of pork rinds, and other edible and nonedible things that are brewed in kettles. But I like it. I like the gadgets, and the soap makers, and the pork rinds, and how there are weird candies and raft rides. My dad likes the bluegrass bands, but sometimes we can't afford the tickets for the week with the bluegrass bands, so we have to go during the festival of crafts. My dad likes this almost as well. He is a man who enjoys a craft, apparently. He especially likes the quilts that are mostly made by hand by what seem like genuine old ladies. I don't know about this thing my dad has for the quilts, but he likes them. Sometimes we drive out of our way to go to a farmhouse where he looks at the quilts a lady makes and then purchases a quilt. He does not use this quilt for a bedspread, but instead has a wooden rack where he displays his quilt. He can only afford one at a time. Quilts are not cheap.

But we like it—we like the Silver City. It is in the mountains. We think it is in the mountains, anyway. On the way we stop and look at the giant Christ. He is perched on the mountain and his arms are stretched out, and you look at him through a telescope from the parking lot of a barbeque restaurant and gift store. This doesn't seem at all odd to me at the time. We get photographed in the parking lot. I am in a romper. I only ever dress in rompers my grandmother makes from what looks like beach towels. Rompers are ideal! Nothing has ever existed more ideal than a romper! I am pleased with myself in my yarn and romper. My brother looks grim. He's not happy about any of it. He is in Adidas and jeans and a baseball shirt, but he has a cowboy hat in his hand because he is about to transition from being into skateboards to being into bull riding.

Then we are suddenly in the Silver City. We walk around in packs admiring the crafts and sometimes going on a ride where you get splashed at the end, which is necessary because it is so hot. It is hotter here than anywhere it seems and smells more like tar, and also more like wood chips, but I receive many things as we walk around, because of the vendors that show you their wares. My dad is the spirit of generosity in the Silver City.

I receive two garters. My dad takes one off the leg of the saloon girl, and then I take one off the arm of the dandy. The saloon girl has fishnets and several tiers of polyester ruffles slit up to her hip socket. She wiggles her shinbone and winks at my dad. The dandy leans down and flexes his shirtsleeve. Even at five, I know that my deal is the less sexy deal. My dandy is a pretty average teenager, and this is the era of the Bruce Jenner physique—fed on cereal, built for knee socks. The dandy is waxed. His whiskers are fake, the shirtsleeves are inauthentic, but when I pull off the garter, the saloon girl catcalls anyway, to heighten the effect. It's a hint: a hint at a world beyond the spectacle, where something adult takes place.

Later we take a tintype. I am bribed with taffy and almond bark. They bribe my brother with down time, bribe him with getting to be alone after. We climb into costumes that are only a front. They velcro in the back, or tie like hospital gowns. The attendants put a big hat on my mother, one with ostrich feathers. They slap a leather vest on my brother and put him in the back row in the picture. My dad is a sheriff or a gunfighter—same costume but with star or without star, depending. I am in a standard Laura Ingalls Wilder farm frock. They take out my yarn, and I get my ponytails made pigtails by some older lady in a similar frock, but one that goes all the way around her. Because she has to be there all day, she gets to be viewed in the round. She likes my dad and talks about how good he looks in the suit. My dad winks at everyone all the time. My mother in her gaudy ostrich hat forgets and smiles when they take the picture, and it ruins the whole thing, so my dad and I do one on our own. It's better: we look like the grim period, the period of hardship.

I LEARN MY RHETORIC FROM
HEE HAW, DESPITE MYSELF.

I remember a show that may not have existed. A variety-type show with Western leanings, but one that was hosted by guitar man Jerry Reed. This was just about the time that he was singing East Bound and Down, and starring in Smokey and the Bandit as sidekick to Burt Reynolds, ultimate mustache. In this show that maybe didn't exist, Jerry Reed came on in a very dapper, flared polyester suit the color of rust or the color of sand and he interviewed musical guests and comedians and movie stars just like he was Dick Cavett. My mother was always going on and on about Dick Cavett, who also came on a show and interviewed guests. But his show seemed to come from New York, and he wore an ascot, and we couldn't even watch his show—it was a show that I don't even remember genuinely airing on our TV, I just know somehow my mother knew all about Dick Cavett. Why? Did it come on after I went to bed? That seems impossible. I had no bedtime. I just stayed up until I became hysterical and had a conniption and then fell asleep while sobbing and choking.

Or, I am little and instead of having a conniption fit and falling asleep choking on my spit, someone reads to me. Someone reads a book with rhyming which is a political allegory. Like Yertle the Turtle. My mother reads it, and then says, 'That's really about Hitler's rise to power.' I am still very scared of Nazis. No one reads me the books about the mice living in a tree and making lots of pies. I have to get these from the public library and then read them to myself, via the pictures. I think I can read already because I have memorized all the rhyming books and because I feel like I can guess what is going on in the books about mice baking pies because the pictures are so detailed. The blackberries are almost as big as the mice themselves and so you get the impression that they could make a lot of pies with even just one blackberry. It makes it seem like it is much easier to be wealthy and live in a multi-tiered mansion inside a tree trunk because having just one thing, like a blackberry, is so abundant.

My mother doesn't like the imaginative aspect of the mice books: they are somehow stupid. For this reason she also hates Smurfs and Ewoks, both beloved by me, and both of which live in vegetative structures. One time, when we are a Nielsen family for a week, my mother writes a letter to go along with our questionnaire saying that all the cartoons on Saturday morning are inane.

Everything on TV is inane. My favorite is a skit on Hee Haw where the barber starts telling stories, and almost immediately there is a tragic aspect: 'Have you heard the latest of my misfortunes and woes?' the barber begins and tells a tragic detail, and the person in the barber chair says, 'That's bad!' and the barber says, 'No, that's good.' And the person in the barber chair says, 'How so?' and the barber then fills in with something that makes the tragic aspect surprisingly lucky, and then the person in chair says 'Oh that's good… ' and then the barber says 'No, it's bad, because… ' and whatever the lucky thing is, turns out to be not so lucky after all, and ends up tragic again, and it loops. That's bad! No, that's good! How so? Because… Oh, Well that's good! No, it's bad! How so? Well because… and it goes on like that 'that's good' and 'that's bad' 'how so' for the entire skit. This cycle could go on forever, an elegant, infinite loop. Everything good is bad, and everything bad is good. My dad laughs a lot at that, because this to him is reality.

I remember this skit and remember the barber as if he is Dennis Weaver. He has a mustache, and a drawl and a dent in his chin, I think. It must have been Dennis Weaver! But my mother, says no, that was Archie Campbell. And I look it up, and she's right, but that is exactly why I don't look things up anymore. They do look alike in a way, same silver swoop of hair, same mustache, same Western-cut jacket, but Dennis Weaver is only about a hundred thousand times more handsome.

In one version of this skit, Archie Campbell, as the Barber, also tells Roy Clark how to get his little boy to go to bed. The little boy is five, and he won't go to sleep for nothing, so the Barber Archie says you can't just tell the same old stories in the same old way, you have to tell the stories backwards, 'in reverse' which meant with letters transposed in the words of the story. He tells the story of Cinder-ella as RinderCella, who lives in 'a coreign fountry with her mugly other and her too sad blisters.' And Barber Archie goes through the whole story, telling it faithfully but with letters transposed in just enough of the words that if you listened closely you could still make out exactly what was happening, if you remembered the story of Cinderella. But by the end, it is all made up language—so that 'the storal of the mory is this: if you go to a bancy fall and you want to have a prandsom hince lall in fove with you, don't forget to slop your dripper!'

Dick Cavett was an intellectual interviewer, whereas guitar man Jerry Reed, on this show that I remember that didn't exist, wouldn't have been an intellectual interviewer, my mother posits. But that's not my memory. My memory of this is that Jerry Reed was a very intellectual interviewer, but all of it in that lovely drawl of his. The way I remember it, Jerry Reed was very intellectual if anyone gave him a chance.

No, that show didn't exist, my mom says. You are remembering Glen Campbell's Goodtime Hour, she says. Was everyone on western shows called Campbell? Campbell is an old-timey name, perhaps? But how is it possible that I remember the Glen Campbell show, when it stopped four years before I was born? Maybe it was on in reruns?

Whatever! Fuck that!—I say to my brother, now, that we are grown. We remember what we remember. Don't let her convince you otherwise, I say to him in the garden between his house and hers, because that is where he lands in life, and so he is susceptible.

When I am little, I love Jerry Reed so much. His songs are genuinely funny, and possibly yes, inane, but I am five and thank god something is inane. And he wears the very flared pants, and he is in the movies where he drives a truck just like my dad. I don't make this connection. I don't make this connection for years. I go on loving Jerry Reed, and thinking he is a great guitarist and great songwriter. I keep it to myself until now except in situations of extreme safety. Some things should only come out in situations of extreme safety. I will only talk about Jerry Reed a tiny bit at a time.

HOYT AXTON IS
FROM OKLAHOMA, AND
SO IS ROGER MILLER.

No one it seems is from Oklahoma except for us
and then I grow up and realize everyone is from
Oklahoma they just don't talk about it after a certain
point or no one talks about them? Cartoons are not
encouraged in my home. They are silly and inane.
But then there is the VHS, and that is something on
my own time, so cartoons are permitted. Everyone
can do what they want, I have the VHS! I am at one
with the VHS! I watch Robin Hood the cartoon,
and it is totally ok! All the characters are animals,
and there are even mice in tea dresses, and there is

the rooster who strolls and sings about Nottingham even though he has a drawl. What is this drawling rooster doing in Nottingham, I wonder?

And my mom even sits in the room with me for part of it because the strolling rooster is Roger Miller, and she loves Roger Miller despite all his songs being inane, and even while the rooster is strolling and whistling she starts in on 'trailers for sale or rent...' and goes on singing for a while, but does anyone say he is from Oklahoma? They do not. Who is from Oklahoma, I wonder? Is anyone? Is anyone famous from Oklahoma?

We sit there and we watch Rockford Files! We watch it religiously, but does anyone tell me James Garner is from Oklahoma? They do not!

Who is from Oklahoma? Maybe murderers? Possibly thieves? Dipshit conservatives? Racists?

I don't find out about Woody Guthrie till I go to college! Till college! And even though we watch all the Western movies at home, and I know Ben Johnson is a famous trick rider, I don't know he's from Oklahoma until college! And then in college I drive every weekend back and forth through Yale, Oklahoma because it's on my route, and I am hyper-aware of Yale because it is a notorious speed trap, and I even get pulled over in Yale, but do not get a ticket because in those days (and still sometimes) I can bat eyes and act dumb and get out of a speeding ticket if the cop is a guy, and through all those travails with Yale, Oklahoma I never know that Chet Baker is from Yale, Oklahoma. Not for years. But where were all those people when I was growing up? I am a grown-up already when one of my friends tells another of my friends, within earshot, 'you have to meet her dad, he is like all the best things about Oklahoma.' She is talking about my dad. It is the first time that I have thought good things about Oklahoma and about my dad at the same time, and I am grown already.

But I remember Della and the Dealer when Hoyt Axton plays it on an episode of WKRP wearing a polyester Western suit that is too small for him.

My dad loves Hoyt Axton. I do not. I think he is not so attractive. He's fat and he wears too-small Western clothes and his hair is gray. I love Dr. Johnny Fever because I love rock and roll, and because I love Jim on Taxi best, because I already love people who seem fried, and have wild hair, and a hippie-type look, and who are wearing jean jackets and dark glasses. At five I love someone fried? They seem more real to me. Johnny Fever wears sunglasses indoors. He always seems hungover. I love Venus Flytrap, too, even though I have never seen a black person except on TV. Venus wears the Porter Wagoner suits but with more style, I think, as if there is only one step between the Porter Wagoner suits and Venus Flytrap suits. There are so many steps! But how would I know, because in Oklahoma we don't totally get it about Super Fly suits, even though my dad is liberal because of being a teamster, and he votes for Jesse Jackson when he runs for candidate, and he enjoys Redd Foxx very much, and we watch Sanford and Son in reruns every day, and sometimes dad listens to the albums by Redd Foxx, and also listens to the Richard Pryor albums, in the same way my brother listens to the George Carlin albums, and I get the impression that things coming out of the record player that are not music but are talking are just way raunchy, because I am often repeating these things with enthusiasm and having my mother say, 'Don't talk raunchy.' I also get the impression that elsewhere in the world there are black people making words and records and movies and TV, they just aren't from Oklahoma, or anywhere around close (and it is not till college that I find out that Ralph Ellison is from Oklahoma City and Langston Hughes is from Joplin, and although, yes, Joplin's in another state, still, we go there for everything, and I have never seen a black person there, and definitely not a famous black poet. What is going on?)

Both my dad and I love WKRP. Is it nice when my dad and I like the same things? I don't know. I don't know about that. I don't love Hoyt Axton, I know that. He is looking fat in that Western suit. I also don't love sports which my dad watches a lot of the time. Sports are the most boring and most cacophonous of all things. Our half house is not big enough for all that sound all the time.

I know when I am in high school, and my friend who is older is over and is playing Steppenwolf and The Pusher comes on and he cranks it up so that you can hear the stereo all the way to the street, my mom and my dad come in from watering the lawn and throw a fit and fall in it because the neighbors are hearing the word 'goddamn' coming from the house at about eleven. It just sounds better that loud. I don't think we any of us know it is a Hoyt Axton song. Because we none of us knew he was from Oklahoma, or talked about it.

My brother knew, I think, because he says, later, in a deadpan way: That's a Hoyt Axton song.

Did he say that? I don't remember. It is much later, in that time when I am looking everything up, like crazy, because I'm scared I'm losing my memory of this place. I want to look it all up and have it confirmed in my mind. Otherwise, you forget.

Then I realize looking it up is what makes you forget. It just erases the memory.

PEARL PEARL PEARL, DON'T GIVE YOUR LOVE TO EARL.

Pearl and Ruby and Opal are sisters, and one of them is married to my dad's friend Urban. Can this be right? Urban? Urbin? I never see it spelled. One of the sisters marries Urban, and one of them marries someone named Roy and the last one (Pearl) marries someone named Earl, and that is not even made up. All those guys are old timers.

My dad has lots of friends that are old timers. This is maybe because he started at the trucking company real young and he was part of a union and in those days the old timers in the union helped out the young guys, and so when the old timers retire, you have to go visit them on the weekends and jaw with them.

The manner of how they jaw is mostly needling. They sit around and needle each other. This is a way of showing fondness and respect and gratitude. The old timers are sometimes so old, and have so many health problems that it's hard to even remember who they are because they aren't around for long. Like the skinny one with the heart problems and emphysema and maybe cancer too, who has a house in Joplin with an apple tree, and a big sloping lawn. When we go in the house, the kitchen counter is just nothing but those orange bottles of pills with childproof caps, but huge ones, big as a Pepsi bottle, almost. I am out the back door like a shot when I see that skinny old timer in front of all those pills. I like the apple tree, though. I like all the apple trees because they are more climbable than almost all other trees because the limbs branch up at the base, and you can usually stand in the center of the branches, and that makes it easier to get into the tree. I just want to get into the trees, and it's harder than it looks, even in the romper, because I have no arm strength.

That old timer with the apple tree does not make it long and so my time with the apple tree is brief. The old timers have wives too, and sometimes after the old timer goes, my dad keeps visiting the widow. But the conversations with the widows are rarely needling. I pay less attention. And when I go with my dad to talk to the widows, he likes me to stay close, because I am a distraction for the widows. I don't get to leave and get into the tree.

But for now Urban is still alive, and he and Opal live in a little house down by the river which has a bench swing on a chain, so when my dad visits Urban I swing on the bench swing and periodically Opal comes out in one of her flowery dresses and gives me a weird kind of baked thing which is old lady baking, so sort of good but also at risk for having a flavor that is all wrong, like raisin or maple. For some reason I am more respectful of Opal than of some other old ladies. For the most part, I like all the old ladies that my dad likes, but I distrust all the old ladies that my mom likes. Why is that? My dad likes the tough old ladies, while my mom likes the soppier old ladies who run dress shops and hair salons.

When the town floods, which is like every spring, it doesn't come quite up into Urban's yard, but you can definitely walk to the flood part without getting out of sight of Urban's yard, so I am permitted to walk to the edge of the flood part while being watched by my dad or Opal from behind the chain-link fence. From here you can see the houses that are underwater. I love to look at the houses that are partly drowned. You see things floating, but next to the edge of a roof, which makes the world seem way more interesting. What is taking place underwater in those houses? Are fish coming through the living rooms? Are water moccasins? Probably. I am way afraid of water moccasins. I'm right about that one.

Everyone in town is poor, but the floodplain people are the poorest, obviously, or they would know better than to be in their bathing suits playing in the flood water, because that is how you get tetanus and probably ringworm too.

I'm not scared of ringworm. My dad is always threatening me with ringworm. If we go where there is a farm cat and there are farm kittens, my dad will not let me play with the kittens because of ringworm. I chase the kittens under the porch and then hide under the porch and play with the kittens anyway. I do not get ringworm. I do not get it until years later and then I get it from a dojo in Pitcher, Oklahoma and my teacher sprays my hand with athlete's foot medicine and it instantly goes away. Seriously? I don't understand about what this worm even is— since it's more like a scab.

My mom is always threatening me with tetanus and I want no part of this since it involves debilitating shots in the arm, and then I can't lift my arm for a week.

My dad really doesn't like it when the old timers go. When Urban goes he looks in on Opal for a long time after, even though I don't think he has much to say to her. There are a lot of widows in the town. All three jewel sisters are widows before long.

CHESTER TREATS
HIS THICK BLOOD WITH
SARSAPARILLA TEA.

I am watching an episode of Gunsmoke with my dad. It is the one where Chester complains of too-thick blood and then everyone has to go out looking for Doc Adams because he's gone missing. Later in the episode, Chester gets stabbed by a horse thief and has to shoot him. The Marshal finds him just after and says, What happened, Chester, did you get shot? No, no, I just got stabbed a little bit is all, Mr. Dillon, he drawls.

I like Festus better than Chester, I say to my dad, in front of the TV.

Yeah, Festus grows on you, I guess, my dad says.

But even by then it is already in reruns, and the reruns have restarted and we are back to Chester already. There's no doubt in anyone's mind that Chester is the way better sidekick for Marshal Dillon. He is just way better. Better looking, better actor, better accent, better character type. Festus is kind of filthy looking, and a little bit creepy, and seems to squint too much. His accent is all wrong in a way that makes people with drawls sound dumb as shit. Obviously, Chester is better. I don't know why I am so contrary.

My father never explains his preference for Chester. But I fix it in my head it is because Chester walks with a limp. But when Chester is on Gunsmoke that is way before my dad walks with a limp, because it is way before he has the stroke that makes him walk with a limp. So why would he care one way or the other about a limp? When Chester is on Gunsmoke my dad is still tall and big and healthy, in boots and jeans with a crease, and he runs and plays basketball and fishes every weekend on the lake in the bass-pro boat, and drives a big truck for a living and drives a smaller truck for fun, and he has a girlfriend who works on the switchboard, and she calls the house sometimes to see if he is there and when my mom answers, that doesn't go well.

After the stroke, a lot changes.

I AM BORN.

I don't like anything that goes in order. I just can't remember what happens when.

My mom says that right before I am born there is a big tornado that damages everything, and that she tries to hide under a chair, but can't fit because she is so pregnant.

Damages what? Everything? Like the house?

No, not the house. But the town. Parts of the town, anyway, she says.

In Oklahoma, there is always a tornado wrecking shit.

The year I am born is the year Gunsmoke ends.

But it makes no difference to Dennis Weaver. He is long gone, and already on McCloud. But McCloud is gone too by the time I am old enough to remember anything, and if it is in reruns, it doesn't come right away. But I hear about it. I hear about how he rides a horse in New York. I wait for the reruns. I know they will come. Reruns are sometimes the future.

SOMETIMES WE TAKE WALKS.

Near our house is the old municipal airstrip which is right next to the new municipal airstrip and hangars for the little planes. My mother's father ran the airstrip for years even as far back as WWII, though I did not ever meet him because he was dead way before I came. He was also a doughboy. My mother has lots of pictures.

My mother's mother is called mom-mom and she lives in half of our house. It's a duplex. It looks like two identical houses stuck together, conjoined houses, or like what polygamist houses in Utah look like. My mother lived in Utah once for a couple of months, and she loved it but my dad hated it and so they moved back to Oklahoma. This is the bane of my mother's existence. But there are no polygamist houses in Oklahoma, because there are no Mormons. At least no one tells me about it if there are.

Mom-mom lets my parents tear down her little white clapboard cottage and build this ranch-style conjoined monstrosity in place of it so everyone has a place to live. She has a whole half, with her own kitchen, and her own TV. If you walk through my room and through my brother's room you get to a hallway that connects to her half of the house, which is the mirror version of our half of the house. Every night for dinner my brother goes in and gets her and walks her through both our rooms while she leans on his arm. She has Parkinson's and though her mind is sharp she has no language. She is paper-thin, and her skin is paper-thin, and she wears a lot of paper-thin house dresses that you can see her spindly legs through when the light is behind her. But for now, she can walk fine if she leans on someone's arm.

The old airstrip looks like a field. It is all split through with Bermuda grass and Queen Anne's lace, and Indian paintbrush and whatever those white flowers are that smell nice but are filled with ants. We take walks there, even sometimes with mom-mom who my mother understands really well even though she's got no language. Sometimes my brother comes and has his skateboard and goes off away from everyone. Every month is a different wildflower in bloom, and I like to snatch and grab everything, regardless of the ants. I like to run off far away from the group, but no one lets me get far without screaming. My mother can't go so fast because she is the arm that mom-mom leans on. She screams bloody murder when I get out of sight in the tall grass and makes my brother come after me which makes him furious. I am never allowed to get far, despite trying. If we get far enough there is a pond. Mom-mom does not go far, so the pond is something very distant, very hard to imagine. I am ready to get far. To get way far from here.

Once during this time, my dad gets the idea to grow a beard and grows a beard. It seems nice, but I don't think it is popular with anyone but me.

Once during this time, my dad gets the idea to buy a motorcycle, and buys one and takes me on exactly one trip on the back of it down the airport road, past the old airstrip and the new airstrip and past the pond to the end of the road with the control tower and all the hangars made of corrugated tin, and there the road just ends in a field, and we get all the way to the end of the road and then have to make a circle, and then he brings me home, and after that no more motorcycle.

LAD, A DOG.

For a while we have a little dog who comes on the walks with us. At night he sleeps in the laundry room. In the daytime he stays outside. I talk to him like he is a person, because I just talk and talk and never shut up. At a certain point this little dog gets a skin disease, and when my mom and my brother and me go on a vacation to Taos, New Mexico, my dad stays home, and the little dog disappears.

This is the year my brother is in a very bad way. He sits in the back of the car for the whole vacation and talks to no one, and I can't remember if he is heartsick or body sick or both. We go all over New Mexico, and especially I like Taos because there are Kachina dolls everywhere, and I am partial to the Kachina dolls. I get one on a beaded necklace and one on a coin purse and one that is just loose. We also go to the pueblo where they still make bread in clay ovens, and you buy the bread, and eat the bread, which is the best bread I have ever tasted before or since, I think. In Taos, there are more mountains than I have seen before, and we go up into the mountains and park near a stream, and I am allowed to wade in the stream in my romper even though it is ice-cold freezing. My brother sits in the car during this. Then, I think, all of us get food poisoned in a fancy restaurant in Santa Fe, and then we drive home. It is hard to imagine how this happens, though, since I only eat croutons from a salad bar. I am going through a phase of only eating croutons. The hard part about New Mexico is finding the croutons. Luckily, I will consent to eating sopaipillas if heavily slathered in honey.

When we get back home, no more little dog. My dad claims he has been poisoned by a neighbor. It seemed unlikely to me, even then.

In those days, folks made it hard for us to love our dogs as we do now, out in the open.

McCloud is from Taos, New Mexico, I am told. It is there he learned to ride a horse.

SOMETIMES I DANGLE
BY MY ARM.

I am always getting pulled somewhere by my arm.
I am dangling like a monkey. I sort of drag my feet
on the ground in my buckled sandals. In my mind it
is always summer for some reason. And then some
one is attached to the top of me by my hand and I
am getting dragged around at a rate that is faster
than I want to go, because I am not going! I don't
want to go! Wherever it is, I don't want to go there!
I am not moving or budging, I am only screaming
and wailing and refusing to pick up my sandals. I
am in a tantrum.

Sometimes I am dangling from my arm in a pleasant way. Someone is dangling me like a monkey, and I will not put my feet down because this is the way the game is played. I dangle by my arm and try to get my feet over my head, or get my feet up onto the body of the dangler. Up onto their waist is okay, but I want to get my feet up onto their chest or even shoulders and drag them down to my level. When they collapse, I have won! Sometimes someone is attached at the hands and someone is attached at the feet and then I am being tossed like a feedbag. Sometimes I am being tossed like a feedbag onto a big bed or onto a trampoline. This is the best, this feedbag-tossing. It is forbidden because my mom says they are going to pull my arm out of the socket.

I don't know who does this sack-tossing thing—cousins probably. There are all sorts of cousins due to my father's brother Fuzz being so much older and having so many kids and then those kids all having kids when they are basically still kids so that sometimes I meet my cousins and they are practically elderly and they have two generations of other cousins beneath them. My dad has other brothers and sisters too, and they all have kids, there's too many to count. Then there is this strange half-family, that no matter how many times I ask about it, I don't understand what it is, because it means my dad's friend Larry is really his nephew, but as a half-nephew? Who has a half-nephew?

Sometimes I am dangled by my arm into the aboveground pool. Because half-nephew Larry is rich from doing electrical work and he has an aboveground pool that is seven feet deep, and when we go over we swim. My dad used to be a lifeguard when he was young, and he takes great pride in teaching/forcing us kids to swim very early on. Aboveground pools are floppy. You can't sit on the edge or sit on some steps, and there is no slow gradation from the shallow to the deep, they just toss you into the trough. And everything disgusting that falls in the trough stays in the trough unless someone takes it out, because there are no drainage systems or cleaning devices, and probably no chlorine either. Probably they fill it with the garden hose. Everything in the aboveground pool—leaves, dirt, bits of mown grass, used band-aids—rotates in a circle like a mild whirlpool.

I float on an alligator, and there is only room for one alligator in the pool at a time, and when I hit the edge, in I go, down and down into the trough with a twang of the reverberating floppy sides, until I touch the smooth plastic bottom of the pool, and I can feel the pebbles and soil and grit and sticks and whatever the pool is sitting on right through the plastic.

Then, swoosh. My dad pulls me up by my arm. Was I drowning? My brother seems unconcerned. My cousins seem unconcerned. My dad seems concerned but undaunted. My mom, who cannot swim, even in the aboveground pool, who had been sitting in a lounger chair in the grass in her white slacks and pink blouse and pink suspenders and buckle sandals perfectly still while I floated on the alligator, now is shaking the floppy sides of the pool and flipping out.

No more aboveground pool. No more cousins tossing me like a sack.

But it is so quiet inside the aboveground pool, at the bottom. You can't hear all the bullshit loud nonsense of all the kid cousins and all the parent cousins and all the grandparent cousins. Inside the aboveground pool there is this muffled sound of the heartbeat and the reverb of the wobbling floppy pool sides, and this is the sound I think that vampires hear when they are really in the moment and they are about to drain their victim.

THE PROBLEM
WITH THE LOOK UP.

I'll tell you the problem with the look up: we lived for a good long while without it and we managed. That sounds like an elderly thing to say. Alas, now I am getting there. I am a woman of a certain age.

But it used to be that if you wanted to know something you had to find the guy who knew the thing and ask. About music especially. I can remember my mother wanting to know who sang that song at the beginning of the film Midnight Cowboy. We had just rented the VHS and watched it together! Yes, I was still very little and this film was rated

X, but to this day I don't know exactly why it was rated X, except for the theme of him being a hustler, or because it was rigged, so that they could avoid giving Jon Voight the Oscar that year so they could instead give it to John Wayne. Jon Voight was always getting screwed out of the Oscar. I was very attached to Ratso in Midnight Cowboy because he was little and sick, and what happens to Ratso in the end, oh my God—gloom, despair, and agony. It was a little much for me.

But we liked the song, me and my mom, and we went around singing it, about how everybody is talking about someone, but he can't hear a word that they are saying. My mother kept saying, 'What was that song called? Who was that song by?' My brother knew. I could tell he knew and wouldn't tell us. He would roll his eyes when we asked. He sent us to the guy who ran the music store in Joplin. It was this one record store where they also sold sheet music and guitar strings, and my brother was already starting to play the guitar, and he was obsessed with buying strings all the time and leaving their little paper sleeves lying around the house.

So we go and we drive the forty minutes, and go into the record store and my mom sings the first few lines of the song to the bearded fellow behind the counter. He looks at us like we are idiots, since the title of the song is the same as the words we have been singing over and over and over again, and because who in the world doesn't know that Harry Nilsson sang Everybody's Talkin'? Anyway, my mom didn't even buy the record, is my memory. All she wanted was to know the answer. We drive home. Later, we tell my brother and he smirks.

There must have been something important in this shaming. For one thing, we never forgot who sang it. And then there was the fact that the smug record store guy got a reason to exist. He held all the cards. You couldn't just look it up, either you knew or you didn't, and either you told someone or you didn't. You got to choose, and if you were like my brother, you got to keep your secrets safe for now.

Come to think of it, I hate this type of shaming. Years and years later when I am in the cool record shop in Denver, and I am milling around in this one section trying to find just this one song by the Kingston Trio and then getting asked by the beardo shop assistant if I need help, and I do because I can't remember the song name, but also I am not wanting to ask anyone because of not being sure that I wouldn't be shamed out of the store by this sort of cute beardo over the Kingston Trio. It was a toss-up. And there I am standing in the bluegrass section, and I just make up a request for a Tom T. Hall album that I already have, and am led to it, with non-response from the beardo, no praise but at least no shaming, and then I purchase it, even though I have the copy that my dad bought years ago, and then I walk out of the store and I never ever go back to that record store again in the entire time I live in Denver. Everywhere I go after that, when I tell people I used to live in Denver, they ask about that really cool record store and if it is still there. It is.

EVERY TOWN HAS ITS UPS
AND DOWNS, SOMETIMES UPS
OUTNUMBER THE DOWNS.
(BUT NOT IN NOTTINGHAM.)

Every year it floods on three sides of our town. I do not know how any town could have floods on three sides, but there it is. My mom says it is because the very rich people who live on the lake to the south of us keep the water levels too high so they can run their speedboats year round, and then every spring, the rains come and we flood, and no one cares because we are all poor. It floods to the south along the river with the park with all the pavilions and the baseball diamonds and the tennis courts

and the Frisbee golf course, and the small municipal (in-ground!) pool. And it floods on the south-
east, behind the high school, and the motels near
the highway. The Townsman Inn and Restaurant
and Lounge has been renovated twenty times in
half as many years, due to floods, most recently to
feature taxidermy animals on a shelf above all the
booths, that stare at you in a menacing way over
your coffee. And the one little tiny movie theater in
town just seems to have water standing in the first
three rows forever and always, and yet it remains
open and we go see movies there, we just don't sit
in the first three rows. It floods to the northeast of
town too, all the way up practically to my Uncle
Fuzz's place, where he sleeps in the daytime while
my aunt Margie sups on sweet n' low. There is the
rust-red creek creeping up the concrete steps of my
Uncle Fuzz's house, while he is sleeping by day,
because he is on graveyard shift his whole adult
life at the tire factory, until he retires early with
asbestos poisoning (from the tire factory).

And I say the rust-red creek, for indeed it is rust and blood red this waterway that cuts through the center of town, because the groundwater has flushed its way through the lead and zinc mines to the northeast of town in Pitcher, the next town over, the ghost town and home of the giant chat piles. What is chat? It is gravel and shale that gets dredged out of the mines. The mines have been shut down for years, but all the chat they dredged out is piled up around Pitcher in giant mounds so that it looks like mountains on the moon, or foothills on the moon, this pale dusty gray range of hills that you can see on the horizon for miles. People run their dune buggies up and down the chat piles, and when I am little my dad goes there to sight his rifles and takes me, and in high school kids go there to hang out and get wasted, and everyone is always waiting to fall in a sinkhole, because what Pitcher is most famous for is sinkholes. The whole town is just perched on a honeycomb of mine shafts, and sometimes a hole just opens up in the middle of town and whatever is there—a truck, a sandbox, a double-wide—whatever it is sitting there just sinks into the earth instantly. When I am in high school and we go to the chat piles to get wasted, anytime someone wanders off to pee, we count in our heads, because if they don't come back in forty-five seconds, we think they have fallen in a sinkhole.

Of course the mines are all closed up by the time I come along, and all the miners are gone mostly because they have died of miner's TB, or have shot themselves when they realized they were dying of miner's TB, like my grandfather did while my father was on the back porch playing in the dirt. (He shot himself in the chest, the source of the trouble!) And now everyone in town works at the tire factory, but even that doesn't last long because it folds, and closes up its gates, but not before months and months of everyone seeing columns of thick black smoke pouring out of its smokestacks, while they burn off the remaining tires.

And yes, this is all toxic, the lead and the zinc and iron oxide in the water and in the chat and in the soil, and the enormous tire factory that has just been fenced off and left to rust and decay in the middle of town, and the crop-dusting of the milo fields and the tanks for the chemicals for the crop-dusting just laying around loose, and the floodwaters coursing through all these things: this makes the whole place a toxic wasteland. We can't play in any of the rivers or creeks, and we really should not drink the water even from the tap, and on days when the black smoke is in the air we shouldn't even breathe if we are outside. (It's no wonder I spend so much time in front of the television.) And everyone from Pitcher for sure has lead poisoning, and it is a running joke about them all being a little bit brain-addled because of all the lead, and if my dad encounters someone in a shop or a restaurant or at the DMV who seems less than swift he says 'I bet he's from Pitcher.'

My dad is very lucky to not work in this toxic town but to have gotten a job at the trucking company one state over because it is a union job and the union is no joke and will shoot anyone that tries to fuck with its members. Well, shoot at. They shoot at the scabs, but they don't shoot the scabs. They perch on an overpass and fire into or around the cabs of the trucks if the scabs cross a picket line. They know how to do it just right, because they are all pretty decent shots because of being veterans and/or having gone through army conscription, like my father. I can see why my dad is loyal to the old timers that made it happen. But even that is not going to last because my dad is going to have a stroke, and then things change a lot.

My mother talks about a time when her uncles and aunts would go down to the railroad trestle bridge and collect freshwater mussels from the base of the iron trestle and *they would eat them* and my dad says, 'Are you kidding me? Not even in the '20s!' But my mom swears it and shows me pictures of her aunts and uncles in antique bathing costumes wading around in the river below the trestle bridge. Their hands are full of something, but it is impossible to say what. Everyone looks beautiful and happy and overdressed in their luxurious black bathing costumes. What the hell happened?

Now we can't even get to that bridge unless we ride bikes for ages and then stumble through a field of burnt-off stubble that if you aren't wearing good sneakers will pierce the soles of your shoes, and then we have to climb around on the decrepit railway and then stumble out on the condemned bridge, and the only thing I know that we ever use it for is for throwing off bottle rockets and watching them explode under the water, but that is a bit later, when I am older. (At the moment, I am only allowed sparklers, and only while chaperoned.)

This is not the sort of thing that would please the Lorax.

I ENJOY A DISLOCATION.

Someone is always chasing me. I am off on a tear and getting chased down for my own safety, so they say. Or I am running from a KISS mask, and I am getting chased as a form of low-level torture. Or I have done something bad, like ripping all the leaves out of a tree I don't like much, and I am being chased down for retribution. God help them if they catch me though, because when I begin a tantrum everything shuts down!

Sometimes I am being chased because my dad thinks I am so sweet and cute that he wants to give me a hug, but I am contrary. I don't know why, exactly, because I like my dad better than anyone, and he clearly likes me best which makes everyone roll their eyes.

I draw a picture of my dad wearing his romper. Yes, my dad wears rompers just like me! Except his romper is more like coveralls with a zipper up the front. His rompers are also made by his mother, and also single colors of fabric and he has a romper in red and in blue and in tan, but not made of beach towels, made of something more durable. He wears his romper for fishing and going to the woods. The blue one is best for the same reasons my blue romper is best—everyone in my family has sparkly blue eyes, despite being part Indian, except my mom. My mom is no-part Indian. But she does have the blue eyes.

So I draw a picture of my dad wearing his blue romper, and I draw the bass-pro boat and then some dogs and cats and a mouse in a tea dress. I leave it for him for when he gets back from fishing, and lo and behold my dad gets back from fishing and finds my drawing of him in his romper and he wants to chase me down and hug me, so there we go, on a tear through the house, me hiding under the bed and him chasing me down, and then almost catching me, but I escape to the living room sofa where I begin my climb to the attic of my mind, up the arm of the sofa, and up along the back of the sofa like a tightrope walker, up and up higher toward the little mouse attic and the little mouse counterpane and my dad gets a hold of my arm and for some reason this time I don't dangle, instead something just pops and that is that. The arm goes floppy. My mom begins to flip out. My brother comes from out of nowhere, and is standing in the room. He stands and stares.

I become hysterical. It is like a tantrum but even worse. My mother becomes hysterical. My father is becoming hysterical, also, but in a more contained way. My brother says, 'Did you guys just break her arm?' and then wanders off down the hall toward mom-mom's side of the house, to play checkers with mom-mom. Then the three of us get bundled into the station wagon, and we drive to Joplin to the emergency room for kids, because even an emergency needs at least forty minutes.

Can't we just go to the hospital by Vesta's house? Vesta is my dad's mom. She is the source of our Indian. She worked in a sewing factory all of her life. Now she lives in town and makes everyone rompers, and lives across the street from what I am quite sure I have been told is a hospital. No way, no way is anyone going to the hospital in this town.

And yes it is all very painful, it must be very very painful, because I scream bloody murder the whole way to Joplin, and continue screaming in the emergency room, and screaming sobbing choking on my own spit in the medical viewing room, and then a doctor comes in. My dad is sobbing and tells the doctor that he thinks he broke my arm. My mother thinks that sounds bad, and people are going to get the wrong idea, and hysterically tries to explain this is not precisely what happened, because dad was chasing me and trying to hug me and I was trying to get away, and that sounds even worse, and the two of them continue talking through the hysteria of what has just happened, and I continue to scream. This emergency room doctor just doesn't even care. I am sitting on a little round swivel stool and he takes hold of the floppy arm with one hand, and spins my little round swivel stool with the other, and as my body spins, my floppy arm stays still, and then the arm pops again, and suddenly feels fine and also works enough for me to smack at the doctor and smack at my mother before I realize I am fine, and also feeling pretty cheery. I receive a lollipop, which is mercifully fruit color! Whew!

My mom is also feeling good: she was right all along, because I *was* going to get my arm dislocated, just not by the feed sack–tossing. My dad is feeling good also, because it turns out he didn't break my arm, and he has learned a valuable lesson: don't chase the kid, don't try to hug the kid. The effect of having a tantrum for several hours is always like this. One feels purged, one feels to be a better person, and one is ready, even, for ice cream.

I PRETEND TO
SLEEP ON A MAT.

Kindergarten, playground of sorrows. For the first time ever, I have to get up early to go somewhere with others, and it is so hard to get up early, because I have been up so late the night before watching the Carson Show.

I enjoy the great Carnac who wears a turban and predicts answers to questions inside sealed envelopes. This is a joke in reverse, because you get the punchline, but then the funny part is the question part of the joke, which comes second, after he opens the envelope. I like this sort of humor: it's all in the arrangement—inevitably whatever comes last is funniest.

On the playground, we play a game called Chasing Boys in which all those who are boys run very fast from all those who are girls. I find it hard to tell the boys apart. None of them have mustaches, which I admire. I find it hard to tell the girls apart, also, in their ponytails which curl into one ringlet and their matching shorty outfits and their ankle socks and jelly shoes. Some girls chase a boy, and should he be caught, attempt to kiss him. If I catch a boy, I involve myself in a fight. This is how I find out often who is tougher than me. Like the boy who must wear a stocking cap on account of having had his head shaved due to lice. He is tougher than me. He is used to being fought and he has toughened up. My toughness does not make me very popular on the playground, but luckily we play only very briefly before we come in for snack and nap.

I don't mind snack, but I do not ever like nap. On rare occasions I am forced to take a nap in my own home, I suspect, because everyone is fatigued of my hamminess and my dancing about in my Wonder Woman underoos, attempting to lift tables. Sometimes I lift these tables, and sometimes there are injuries. On such instances, when I am forced to take a nap, I do not sleep. I only pretend to sleep, while climbing on my canopy bed like it is a jungle gym until my brother slips into the room and begins to breathe like Darth Vader and I run screaming through the house in my underoos. Sometimes, this ends in an actual nap following the dénouement of the Vader tantrum. I have screamed and sobbed and thrashed about and have choked on my spit and begun to hyperventilate and this ends with me in a dark room at twilight, finally sleeping, against my will, falling to the will of others.

In kindergarten, I am told that I must nap on a mat, so I pretend to nap there, in the dark of the room, but I do not nap, instead I count the acoustic tiles on the ceiling, and then meditate upon the creatures on the bulletin board that are made of letters.

They are the alphabet, but they are also individual colorful monsters, with claws and fur and teeth and sometimes horns. Each monster letter can sort of cavort his or her way into a word, but the monster letter always begins the word, and the following letters are just regular pieces of font. I take a particular interest in the monster J, which is my special letter for myself and my dad. She is purple and furry and has a single eye with batting lashes, and clawed hands and feet, and a lolling tongue. The D is also okay, I guess, even though it is for my mom and my brother. The D is orange (not my favorite) but has horns and leopard spots. I cannot yet read the words, but I can already see the hierarchy. The other letters are nondescript. They are pawns in the game of the monster letter. The monster letter exacts her will on others of her species; she is the master of the word!

I WILL NOT EAT A SQUIRREL.

When my dad and his brother Fuzz go to the woods together, they come back with a string of squirrels. My dad cleans the squirrels of their little jackets and trims them of heads and feet, then pops them into freezer bags for later. For what later, I wonder, since my mother is never going to cook these squirrels and we are not going to eat these squirrels, and since my dad would almost starve I think if someone did not cook for him, the freezer fills up with squirrel meat.

But the freezer is always so full of meat! My father drives an hour away to a place where he knows a butcher who will give him a whole side of beef for a very good deal, and so we drive there, and I play in the front of the shop even though the store is closed and the lights are mostly off inside all the meat cases, while my dad loads very many coolers with very many white packages of meat. At the front of the shop, there is a little cow holding a chalkboard in his hoof that has the specials for the day. I erase the specials and draw on the cow board. I draw a cow that looks similar to the cow holding the board, and then a little mouse in an outfit, and then a squirrel carcass, but there isn't enough room to fit the squirrel carcass onto the little chalkboard so I take the chalk to the floor of the shop and there I paint my master-pieces, on the floor of the shop until my dad comes in and snatches me up, and that is that last time we get a deal on a side of beef!

That meat fills up the freezer, but also we eat the meat every day, so there is a beef theme in our lives that season, whereas mostly there is a chicken theme or a fried-vegetable theme. My mother buys a grinder and then grinds the meat because meat that is loose is more versatile than meat that is in a large chunk, it seems, now made loose it can become burgers or chili or taco meat or sloppy joes or burritos or patty melts or spaghetti sauce or Swedish meatballs or can be helped with a box of helper. No one it seems is allowed to tire of the beef season. Except now my father is gone almost all weekend fishing and going to the woods, and he comes home with the fish and cleans many fish and puts them into the freezer bags, and then comes home with the string of squirrels and cleans the squirrels and puts them in the freezer bags, and not only is our freezer full now of meat and fish and squirrels, so full there is almost no room for the many ice cube trays that are necessary to make the sugary ice teas that everyone consumes daily in enormous quantities, but mom-mom's freezer is also full of meat, even though she eats like a tiny bird, so she is not going to help make a dent in all that meat. And my mother is getting a little bit tired of coming in from her part-time job as a secretary and having to cook all that meat and sometimes it just seems like no one is happy.

While my mom prepares the meat, she watches Donahue. Donahue is the most boring of all shows, so I must flee. My father is not home yet, because he is on a new work schedule that means he has to be up at 4 a.m. and out of the house to go get in the trucks and drive the trucks all over till very late in the evening and sometimes he is not home even in time for M*A*S*H, and so he sleeps with the radio on all night, because somehow this helps to either make him sleep or helps to keep him from sleeping too much so it's possible to wake up so early to work so long? I'm not sure. But the radio is always on in their bedroom, and sometimes, in the daytime, to escape the sound of Donahue I hide in the gap between the big bed and the wall, and the music is playing southern nights, or hunka hunka burnin' love, and even with this contemporary soundtrack, I am able to imagine this gap between the bed and the wall, where I am nestled in shag carpeting is actually a straw bunk inside a snowbound cabin, and I am an orphan who has wandered in the wilderness and is starving and suffering from fever, but I have been found nearly perished in the snow by an unknown couple who are benevolent and willing to save me from scarlet fever via nourishing broths and they are quite happy to raise me in their home. There is only bear meat to eat of course, but it doesn't matter, because I can't eat any solid foods due to the scarlet fever, I can only have someone spoon me broth. In my mind I picture myself partly as a girl, and partly as a little fox. Sometimes, I hide there in the shag rug, for some time, until someone notices I am missing and comes and accuses me of something, because why would I hide there in the bedroom, in a dark trench between the paneling and the comforter if I hadn't done something and wasn't awaiting retribution? I just want to be alone in my straw pallet, with my restorative broth, and my little pioneer fox family for a little longer while my mom is watching Donahue and cooking dinner. But then the supper hour dawns and all are summoned to the loose meat, and the table that is covered forever and always with the oilcloth with giant pink roses.

And my brother still escorts mom-mom to the table through our two rooms, but now mostly he leaves and does not stay at the table. As often as not, no matter the form, the loose meat is served on white paper plates, layered with white paper towels, which are there to soak up the extra loose meat grease. You scoop the loose meat (as if for taco) right off the paper toweling, and you scoop a charred lump of formed loose meat (as if for burger) off the paper toweling, etc. When eating the loose meat, you eat also very much paper towel. Chili and other sorts of moister loose meats are served in their cooking pots.

Sometimes, instead of hiding in the trench in the bedroom, I hide under the table, under the tent of the oilcloth. Under the table you can see that the table is actually made of wood and is sort of fancy as it is Ethan Allen from the early American collection which is my dad's favorite collection of furnishings in dark walnut wood. Under the table you can also see where my brother has carved many things in retribution against the table, and drawn many pictures of violent retribution being enacted on members of the family.

I can still hear Donahue from under the table, though, and so sometimes I must just go to the out of doors and swing on the little red swing and play with the small dog who is getting a little mangy from his grass disease. One time I come in from playing in the out of doors, and my dad is home from work, and my mom is in the kitchen with him and someone has cooked a squirrel. I don't know who, my dad I guess? Or my mom for some reason? My mom is standing with her arms crossed. My dad tries to get me to eat the squirrel. I nibble on the small squirrel limb, which looks like a tiny drumstick by the time it is cooked in the pan. Stringy. Oily. Gamy. I hurl the little drumstick. I will not be eating any more of that squirrel. What kind of person is the kind of person who hunts squirrels? A sick, backwards person.

Okay, okay, no one's making you eat the squirrel. My mother looks smug and victorious. My father looks wounded. My brother is nowhere to be seen.

FOLKS TEND
TO KILL THEMSELVES.

My father has a friend called Gene who was in Vietnam. My father fell between the wars, and he had done his conscription already so he wasn't drafted. Gene was just enough younger than my dad to be drafted. Gene is an oddball, my father says, because of Vietnam. How so? My father says they dropped agent orange right on him, and that he walked through the jungle drenched in agent orange, and that affects a guy in the head.

How does it affect a guy in the head? This is unclear to me as a kid. Gene is funny, and when he comes over he tells me jokes and acts like he sees kids. So many of the old timers just don't even see the kids, so when the oddballs come around I like how they tell jokes and entertain me and heap attention upon me, because I am hammy and I like all the attention. Gene is cousins with several of my dad's other friends including Urban, who is an old timer, and Tommy who has a terrifying chicken farm. My dad takes me once to Tommy's and I step into the chicken house, and see all the zillions of chickens kind of piled up on top of each other, screeching and smelling to high heaven, and entangled in a bunch of net-cage, and it's hard to tell where the one chicken begins and the next chicken ends and I think, O holy hell, no way am I going back in that chicken house, and I scream and cry a little, and have to be assuaged with a peacock. The peacock is a novelty bird and he walks around loose on the ground rather than being semi-caged and piled high into an oversized stinking Quonset hut, and so I can follow the peacock at a discreet distance without panicking myself or others and eventually someone's wife (Tommy's?) brings me a feather she has collected from him, and I feel assuaged from the chicken trauma.

So I don't like Tommy much, and I like Urban fine, but he is an old timer and not long for this world. Gene is the best of the bunch, I think. He is also friends with my dad's brother Fuzz and all of them dress in camouflage and go to the woods on their off days together and hunt squirrels or get in the speedboat and go to the lake, or get in the flat-bottomed boat and fish, or sit together at the cafe, though this I think of as happening later, after the stroke when things have changed.

(The cafes where my dad and his friends and all their old timers sit and drink coffee and eat sweet rolls are not quite the same as the cafes in France where you go and drink coffee or drink a diabolo menthe. However, they are both places where old men and medium-old men and even youngish men go to sit for hours and drink coffee and mingle with each other, and they are both places that seem to close up in the evening time. The cafes where my dad goes have the hard-faced waitresses however, and you don't have to find a guy to pay the bill after you are finished like you do in the French-type cafes. Also the hard-faced waitresses are supposed to come and pour a million cups of coffee endlessly whereas in the French-type cafes you buy one coffee and if you want another coffee you have to find a guy and ask for another coffee. But all this I learn much later, when later there are other places I have been.)

But I have to be careful to stay on track, because this is the story of how Gene just suddenly was dead, after a hunting accident, on a Saturday morning when my dad is out fishing or in the woods, and while I am watching inane cartoons. This is before the Ewoks, I think, so I have been watching a cartoon where there are all these dogs that travel around Europe and parts elsewhere in a pack led by a spotty dog called Petey who is looking for a little boy who owned him once. I like the taller dog called Bandit who wears a neckerchief and is scrappy. Petey is more the intellectual of the group, and he is always just almost finding his boy, but his boy is such a world traveller, and the two have been separated by nefarious means, obviously, and so there is a lot of near-miss, and then in the meantime Petey will solve a crime or help out a child in some way while also learning something about history, such as in the episode I've just been watching in which Petey and the gang stow away on a passenger boat and arrive in Berlin in search of Petey's boy, and they see him, like at a distance across the docks, but then he gets carried off, and instead they have to help a little girl who is on one side of the Berlin Wall reach her grandmother who is perhaps sick or in danger on the other side of the Wall, and this involves all the dogs swimming a lot. Perhaps the Berlin Wall is on the edge of a river? Or perhaps Berlin is on the ocean? A lot is unclear about the further adventures of this dog called Petey. It's my favorite inane program.

Then, just as Fat Albert is about to begin, my mom comes in and says Gene has been killed in a terrible hunting accident while on a hunting trip with Uncle Fuzz in Germany, and we must be careful how we tell Dad. How *we* tell Dad? Yes, we must be careful. Then Dad comes in from the woods, and is still in his camouflage which smells of Deep Woods Off, and still carrying his gun case when my mother shout-blurts that Gene has had a terrible hunting accident and is now dead and my father says without much energy, 'That was no accident' and then has to sit down. He sits down and holds his head for a bit, and scrunches his face like perhaps he is going to cry but doesn't and this is the way I often picture my dad crying in a dry, scrunchy way, and so in later years when I remember an image of my dad crying, like after we are fighting or after Vesta dies or after he finds out things he doesn't want to find out, I picture this moment, but perhaps he was not scrunch crying in those other moments, but was in this moment, or perhaps he scrunch cried in those other moments but not in this moment.

I would like to be taken to the miniature golf course, please, but it is not going to happen, so instead my mom takes me and my brother to a department store in Pittsburg, Kansas which has a third-floor balcony with a couch on it that overlooks the whole store and there is a basket of picture books by this couch which I like, and my mom can shop on the ground floor for lots of Garanimals outfits for me, while I sit on the couch, and periodically she waves up to me, or makes me come down to try on outfits. My brother leaves and goes to a music store down-town and he comes back later with a bag of strings and sheet music and then sits in the back of the car. After the shopping is done, and we are driving back the forty minutes from Pittsburg, Kansas, my mom says that we have to be careful about what we say about Gene having killed himself, because Dad's dad killed himself but he doesn't remember and we have to be careful about that.

If Dad doesn't remember, my brother asks, then how do you even know?

Because Vesta told me, my mom says, and that is that, and now we all know that some folks tend to kill themselves, and that it is possible to forget, and that such things are a delicate matter.

I DREAM OF JERRY REED.

I am totally grown up, and living with someone, when I have this dream that I am at an event at a coliseum which has two levels. A kind of concrete stadium on the edge of a lake. I've come to watch a performance, and I think I look great. I am dressed very sexy. I seem to know someone is going to be there. And someone is: Jerry Reed! A bit older than he was in Smokey and the Bandit, but not much older, and he seems thrilled to hang out with me, a much younger woman. He sits with me at the edge of the lake, very sweet-like. We hold hands.

Then I see a couple of friends, a poet and his wife, but they are on their way somewhere else. It's the poet's birthday, and I wish him a happy birthday, and kiss both him and his wife and then they get up to leave with hardly a word. Why are they going so soon? I ask Jerry. He shrugs. Perhaps they disapprove of me being with Jerry who is pawing me and making jokes and cracks; I mean everyone knows I live with this other guy (the one in real life).

From there I go with Jerry Reed to the upper level of the coliseum. It reminds me of this bullfight arena in Arles, in France, where I went once, the first and only time I ever saw a bullfight. But there is no bullfight, and I think that maybe where I am with Jerry Reed is not a bullfight arena, but is more clearly the ruins of the fortress structure on the edge of the Mediterranean in Cassis (also in France) where I lived for a few months once (in the real world). The fortress ruin is where I often walked alone, in the afternoons, to a place called the Tennis Club, which was an outdoor cafe which in France means it was open until late afternoon and then it closed up. You just sit and drink a coffee and when you are done, you have to find the guy who runs the cafe and give him some money. Presumably, this cafe was also somewhere you could play tennis, but I never actually saw any courts or anything, or anyone dressed to play tennis. There were no courts, in the real France to my knowledge. In the dream, there were courts. In the dream, it is dark as Jerry and I walk around the old fortress and the Tennis Club has already closed for the day, and all the chairs are up on the tables, and the awnings are rolled in, and the blue and yellow umbrellas are shut. We walk to the end of the fortress, and end up on a secluded little beach below, where Jerry attempts to seduce me. He promises me that the guy I live with will never find out. This makes sense of course, because the guy I live with exists in the real world and Jerry Reed only exists in my mind. We do it. Just dissolve right there in the dark on the beach, in the tiny little cove. He's pretty good, is all I remember; he's better than

I would guess because he shuts up, and stops with the jokes and is very present.

Later someone finds my body and, oddly enough, my dog's body, on this little shore, but by then I am asleep and my dog is asleep, and Jerry is long gone. I try to convince the authorities it is not my body, and that even if it is someone else's body, Jerry is not involved. That's how it goes in dreams. You are both dead and asleep and you are awake outside your dead/asleep body and you still have to make all your own excuses. It's like I never stop trying to defend myself, even after I'm dead in the dream. And I'm trying to defend Jerry Reed too, and what do I know maybe he did kill me? My poor dog is just along for the ride.

I pursue Jerry to another town where he is performing at another stadium in a costume, dressed like a rodeo clown. He seems pretty put off by my turning up a second time. He is not interested in having me follow him like a groupie, but then I explain the situation. I mean really! Who the hell does he think he is? He wasn't that good! What an ego. Anyway, the situation in the explaining seems too restrictive. Too many anxieties about whether or not it was my body I saw there, washed up on the beach. I give up. Jerry invites me over for lunch at his house, which is close by luckily. His house is very nice, with a lovely central staircase!

Do you think we are still in France? I wonder, I wonder what kind of a mind takes Jerry Reed out of his element and sticks him in a coliseum in France and nearly gets him arrested for double murder (humanimal double homicide, I call it in the dream).

DISLOCATION/RELOCATION.

So all of it just stopped. One day, we turn on the TV and no more Marshal Dillon and Chester/Festus, no more hayrides, no more kissing cousins and Daisey Dukes and no more barber shops and no more Mandrell Sisters, and no more pea-patch Paw Paws, and no more fat men in Western suits and no more Opry and vests that sparkle and light, and no more hillbillies and no how-w-deee and hats with price tags, and no more green acres, and no more houses on the prairie or on the banks of Plum Creek or anywhere rural. Just gone, like that. Overnight? It seems it. And no more drawl, except for Dallas entrepreneurs and decadent Southern capitalists, or the classy kind of drawl of women interior designers from the Deep South, the drawl that is reminiscent of plantation life and white columns and all those films from the '30s where southerners were played by Brits, and so the accent is half-drawl half-Laurence Olivier. Not my culture, I can tell you that! My mother always said the easiest dialect for actors to slide between was polished British English to slow sleepy Southern like Savannah. She imagines this is because that is where the accent actually comes from. Where does my mother get this kind of information? And why does she still purvey it?

And shortly thereafter, the truckers were gone as well. And there goes McCloud, on that horse that he rode in New York. I see him there meandering off, disoriented, tired like at the end of Shane, but the street sign says Hill Street, and there's nothing but cabs.

The rural purge. It's a term for what happened to the TV. And yes, I looked it up. It's real. That's the other problem with the look up: you are reminded that culture is ruled by the whim of a few.

And there were reasons to see it go. There were definite reasons, and in fact perhaps it is just best forgotten, all that inane rural culture that paraded its spectacle across the airwaves. There were reasons to hang down one's head in shame, to hang down one's head and cry. Reasons it made my Ms. Magazine mother wince, and reasons that it made it hard to imagine anything but an all-white world except through parody, or stereotype, or worse. There were reasons to get those girls out of those short shorts and into some power suits and shoulder pads, and there were reasons that as soulful as Charley Pride might have been when he came on Hee Haw, it didn't make sense in a world where there was Curtis Mayfield or Marvin Gaye. How could it?

But what came instead after this pogrom of the rural? What were they making room for in all those time slots? If it was M*A*S*H, I understand. I understand about M*A*S*H. If it was to make room for the black families, I get that too, but why did everyone have to live in a penthouse or a brownstone or in Bel Air? Even the breweries and the pizzerias and the junkyards and the auto mechanics are going away. Everyone is moving up! Moving up to champagne wishes and caviar dreams, and rich women in ski lodges in Denver fighting over their husbands' and ex-husbands' private jets while wearing fur coats. Upwards on oil wells. Up, up up to the sexy and incestuous saga of a wine-growing dynasty in Napa with their own family crest! Onward from the dust bowl, onward to Fantasy Island! I too can spend my life perpetually on a cruise ship! I too can live in a vineyard, like my betters.

We must, we must, we must move up, move out, remove ourselves from the country! No one wants to see stories about poverty and dirt and hardship on a regular basis. It's a buzzkill.

THE WORLD OF THE LAKE.

How it begins is that he is gone. He is gone more and more. Where gone? Gone fishing. Where gone? Gone to the woods. Gone to the lake to his sister's house.

The switchboard girl calls and even she can't find him. Where is he? He's gone and gone some more. Gone for whole weekends, and then he comes in so late at the end of the weekend that Starsky & Hutch is on and I am hardly able to concentrate on him at all.

One day, he turns up in the afternoon while I am at home by myself. By myself but with my brother, because sometimes my brother is in charge of me but in the way where I never see him. I remain still in front of the TV, he remains in his room where there is another, smaller TV, and a trundle bed with a train set inside the bottom drawer instead of another bed.

My father appears suddenly out of nowhere and suggests I come to the lake. We go to the lake where his sister lives. Her name is (honest to God) Feral. My father's sister is named after a wild thing, and indeed she is famously a wild a thing: a cocktail waitress! Well, no longer a cocktail waitress, but once a cocktail waitress. But she is so much older than my dad, they are further apart even than me and my brother. She is old enough to be his mother, and in fact much later I am told, perhaps she really is his mother, and Vesta just covered for her. It's hard for me to know. I only meet her once or twice.

And by hook and crook Feral, the former cocktail waitress, has come to own a house on the lake, the coveted lake of the rich, the one kept so high that it floods our town. At Feral's house there are fine furnishings from the Early American Collection with wooden arms and wooden footstools, and there are lots of bits of shining driftwood, and out the windows is a view of the still high lake, and the trees surrounding them. There are also lots of fancy rocks lying around in a decorative fashion. I am not allowed to touch them. Not allowed to touch the rocks? They are rocks! No, they are special rocks. Okay, I say, I see. But I do not see. I resist a tantrum because I am rarely permitted to go to the lake where my father and his sister have a secret special world. On that occasion I play upon the rocks outside, the rocks that are okay to touch, near the water's edge. My mother would never let me go so close to the water's edge. She can't swim at all, and she thinks everyone is on the verge of a drowning all the time. Here at the lake, I enjoy a special freedom.

Then I am returned home, where my mother has been waiting in an ever-increasing panic, and where my brother sits smugly on the sofa, his arms crossed. He shrugs. Not his problem. My mother screams hysterically, and forbids my father to ever take me there again. Then, she tells me if he tries to take me there, I should never ever go. What happened there? Was that switchboard girl there? I should never go there. I should revolt! It is not safe there! It is dangerous. Feral is a drinker!

And so it continues, that he is less and less in the home, and more and more in the secret world of the lake. The dark, deep, still cool lake. Floating, perhaps, in a flat-bottomed boat. Or perched on a bench very near to an arrangement of fancy rocks. What does he do there? He is not a drinker. He is a teetotaler forever and always. Drinking is a weakness, he says. He says it often. Drinkers are weak people. Perhaps he doesn't feel this applies to his sister, Feral, former cocktail waitress and keeper of the lake. I am not ever again invited.

THE STORY OF THE STROKE.

And suddenly he is gone completely. With the help of Feral he has found his own little house on the lake and he is gone there and there he shall stay! My mother begins crying. This goes on for several days. I desire a grilled cheese sandwich. One cannot be had! I cry and scream but no more loudly than my mother. Eventually my brother comes and makes the grilled cheese sandwich. He hands it to me on a saucer without speaking.

It goes on like this for a time. How long a time? A very short time. My father's escape is so very brief. He is gone for only one week. Then, one day,

I come home from kindergarten and something is very wrong. More wrong even than it has been in the week of the weeping mom.

I have had a hard day, that day at kindergarten, very much in keeping with so many of my long, dark days of kindergarten. I have arrived late as usual, because I have not been able to awaken. I have had altercations on the playground, and I have been accused by my teacher of being mean to the church girls, even though the church girls are classically the meanest girls on the planet. Yes, I have been mean to the horrid church girls, but not mean enough! Not by a mile! Afterwards, I have been given a snack, and I have not enjoyed my snack. And, I have been caught talking during nap to the lice boy. For talking during nap, I am made to sit in an isolated shaming location known as 'the box,' which is for solitary confinement and contemplation of wrongdoing. Only I love the box, which is like a small safe cave, and I have begun to chat to myself in the box about those mice in the tree and without noticing have chatted louder and louder regarding these mice, until, in vexation, my teacher drags me out of the box by my arm and my name is added to a chalkboard. This is the precursor to a collective punishment, for if one's name appears on the board and then wrongdoing continues, one's name receives a *check mark*, and the entire group is punished in some incomprehensible way by the appearance of this check mark, incomprehensible in part because it never happens, because a name is added as a precursor, but then the collective shaming begins, so rarely does the name have an opportunity to continue in wrongdoing. And also, we are only there for a few hours, and we can barely even read our own names. In a way, how could it ever go so wrong as to require a check mark? Such is the danger of the marked name, however.

But I manage; I survive the hardship, and I have made it through without a check mark, but when I emerge from the building I have not been picked up by my mom in the cul-de-sac of hovering cars. I have instead been picked up by the mother of my fanciest friend, the one who lives in the house where Dennis Weaver's wife grew up. She has picked me up, and has taken me to Dennis Weaver's wife's house, and she has given me a snack of fine waxen biscuits and she has kept me there till nearly suppertime, and then she has driven me back and dropped me at my home where something is going wrong. What has happened?

The stroke has happened. The stroke has struck in the night! My father in a little house on the lake has suffered an aneurysm followed by a hemorrhage. This aneurysm followed by a hemorrhage has been accompanied first by pain, then by incomprehensible rage demonstrated in the utter demolition of the little house on the lake, and this was followed by disorientation in which some sort of a call has been placed to someone, perhaps Feral, perhaps Fuzz. My father is now in intensive care in Joplin, land of all things. Not so far, only forty minutes.

What is the nature of a stroke? It is hard to say. Something in the brain ceases to flow perhaps? Or begins to flood its boundaries? There is a leak, a surge or a swelling. There is a point at which language stops, and perhaps will not begin again. But this is not the worry on anyone's mind.

What happens next? Many things which do not happen ever. The phone begins to ring and ring—it is sometimes a doctor, sometimes an uncle, sometimes the switchboard girl who my mother shouts at—don't call here! Then my mother disappears, and returns with Vesta! Vesta in our home? This never happens. Mom-mom lives in our home. Vesta lives elsewhere in a little house on central street with a flooded basement, and a large pecan tree in the yard, where she is forever and always taking in sewing, and washing, and ironing, and making the whole neighborhood rompers.

Then my mother leaves again. Leaves us there, my brother and I, with Vesta who attempts to offer me a food. I rebuff the offering. My brother appears and is persuaded to make me a sandwich. I accept the sandwich. Then Vesta draws me a bath of an inch of cool water and places me in it for five minutes. I do not take baths in an inch of water! I take baths in several cubic feet of water, and I take these baths interminably, until quite chilled and puckered and beside myself, because I have been developing whole underwater fantasyscapes with various of my aquatic playthings, and also perhaps because I have been forgotten in the bath. Perhaps because Vesta remembers the dust bowl, she believes a bath is an inch of water and it lasts five minutes. Then, unbelievably, horrifically, I am put to bed. There is still light in the western sky. I lie in the bed in horror. I have never been put in bed so early.

That night, my brother does not breathe as Vader, nor does he pursue me in a KISS mask. I long for this familiar terrorizing. I begin to sob and choke on my spit. I am unattended. I lay for some time in this state of sob. Then, as with a tantrum, the sobbing passes and I sleep.

The next day, I am removed. I am removed to a neighbor's house.

We pack my bags in the living room, and then my mother bundles me. I will be fine here, my brother says to Vesta. Just leave me. I will be fine. And there he remains with mom-mom, who needs looking after a bit, not nearly as much as me.

The neighbor is called Agnes, who is an old lady who is the mother of my mother's best friend from childhood. I know her well enough. My mother takes her to the grocery store on Saturdays and I ride along in the car and then sometimes, in the grocery store, I choose to follow Agnes around rather than following Mom around. Agnes's husband died of the miner's TB years ago, and he was well-beloved, and in her little house just blocks from my own, there are sepia-tone pictures of him all over the walls.

Agnes, for some reason is someone I do not mind. Why? She is perhaps just simply benevolent. She is perhaps just a kind old lady. Yes, she is the perpetrator of the German Chocolate ice cream. She also tries to perpetrate lime sherbet, most hateful of all fruit flavors. But otherwise, I like her. I will now live with her. I will sleep in the bed with her, even though the bedspread is made of crochet.

And so I do. For what seems like some time. But how long is some time? My mother passes through for an hour only in the afternoons, one hour per day, or one hour every other day. At night she sleeps on a cot somewhere. Where? In a hospital. Or in a waiting room of a hospital, it is unclear.

My brother is I don't know where, but perhaps he has remained with the home. Or perhaps he is wherever the other one is, the one that I have now nearly forgotten. The stroke victim. This goes on for so very long.

I am five. It's probably only a few months or slightly more. Any time is a very long time, and all that time is time in the memory of an unformed mind. Be careful, my therapist reminds me, now, in these much later days: those may be screen memories. What are screen memories? I ask. The memories that we put in place to protect us from worse memories.

Worse memories? There could be, somewhere within me, worse memories? Worse than this thing where my dad once was, and then was not? Or was not quite not, but was very nearly not—hovering on the verge of not. Was removed, or removed himself, and then was removed all the more, as if in punishment for his first removal?

Screen memories. And so that little dog that had adventures in Berlin replaces the story of the suicide of my father's friend—or the story of the suicide of my father's friend becomes confused and my father is someone now in it, inside the memory, and his gun is being propped in such a way near him so as to make this notness seem accidental, unplanned. Perhaps my father was, after all, on that hunting trip in Germany, and is dead in the same way, as it seems, he has been erased.

THE TOPOGRAPHY OF A TREE.

At Agnes's house there is a picture of a tree which is not a picture but which is more a raised surface, a topography of a tree, made with quilled paper leaves, tightly coiled and glued to the wooden surface, in yellow and orange and gold, and there is a thick, knotted trunk in brown and gray quilled swirls, interlocking, and the tree stretches its limbs out toward a series of clouds, and in the clouds are various names, and so the tree of her family is recorded in a kind of white calligraphy in the margins of the frame. She is, she tells me, a daughter of the revolution.

I would like to draw such a tree for myself, but we do not know all the clouds to fill in. Honey, no one knows much about your dad's people, she says. Agnes remembers a few things about my mom-mom and her husband, and that is about it. She knows nothing about any other of the people we come from. They are all dead or gone.

Agnes has many children and grandchildren. The youngest grandchildren are my brother's age, and they are also responsible for lots of sack-tossing of me over the years. I like them because they are fancier than us. Their father works for an oil company and they have a nicer home and nicer things, and the girl looks more properly like a girl from TV and the boy looks like a boy who will go to college, and later does.

They ask after my brother. I have no information. Everyone in Agnes's family calls my brother by his first name and his middle name, which I know he hates because his middle name is my dad's first name. It is also part of my own name. There are a few too many namesakes.

While I stay with Agnes, everyone comes to see me on the weekends and keep me company. Or perhaps they come to protect her from my famous tantrums. I am mostly tantrum-free with Agnes, but that is in part due to the shaming on the part of her older grandkids. They shame me, and then are very nice! Shame then niceness! Sometimes they boil me an egg and remove the yolk, which I do not like, though I like the rubbery white. This is an act of shortchanging my tantrum by just doing the thing that I want while shaming me for wanting something difficult! I learn this important lesson that getting something you want is never free of shame!

Sometimes, these grandchildren color a picture with me, but they like me not to press so hard on the crayons. Why do you make it so dark? It looks better when you color it in lightly. I like it dark, I think it looks better when the thick layer of wax on the page makes the colors shine. They are dark and darkly lined, and therefore each part is distinct. I like this better, even though it is messy and sometimes tears the paper. What do I care?

Sometimes, they put my hair in hot rollers, which almost any child in the world would mind, but I do not, because I am already seeking a kind of more contemporary beauty in the form of little matching shorty outfits and jelly sandals and long loose waves of elegant hair. Farewell to homemade rompers!

A GROTESQUE BUT
SENTIENT CREATURE.

One day, after some time passes, my mother appears with my brother at Agnes's house. She has come to take me to visit my dad. I had forgotten there was one. How the time flies!

He is in the hospital in Joplin. There have been many surgeries, I am told in the car. Many surgeries on his brain. And many surgeries involve many stitches and many restraints, and on one evening not so long ago, he has torn free of his restraints and attempted an escape from his bed, but in so doing, has crashed and fallen and split open his many stitches, and this has involved many more surgeries and many new stitches. I am warned that he struggles with words. I am warned that he has changed.

We arrive at the hospital, and my father is there in his pajamas and in his red Hawkeye bathrobe in a chair, and although he can sit up and although he seems alert, he has not yet fully regained language, and he is not, to say the least, anything like my dad. He is skinny, far too skinny, and his head is shaven and covered over with red, emblazoned embroidery. He is a patchwork doll now.

He cannot hug. To hug him will hurt him. Besides, I am scared of him. He is a fright, a monster. I hide behind a chair.

Stop that woman calling my house, my mother says, and then we leave.

ONWARD, TO
TREMBLING MOUNTAIN.

You don't remember, my brother says to me when he is driving me to the airport. You're so lucky you don't remember.

Yes, I am grown. All grown, with a home of my own (I think!) and a husband (of sorts) and a job (of even lesser sorts). My father has just been through an operation for colon cancer that has not, to say the least, gone well. They have taken away more of the colon than they were supposed to take, and now he has to have an apparatus attached to him, but little difference it makes since what has really happened is they have discovered the cancer is everywhere, even in the lungs, and he has only a few months left to live. Do I know this yet? I half know this. I find out more while staying in a chateau above Montreal where I am going, if I can just make this flight, and my brother is driving very fast, but it is far, it is far away, like everything.

For now, I know the surgery has gone badly. I have seen him, and I have been with him after the surgery, but I have not stayed. I could only stay for the surgery. The surgery was supposed to go well. It did not. Now I must go to Montreal, and from there to Mont-Tremblant, the ski village where they speak French. My sort-of husband is taking us to a beautiful chalet with a swimming pool and several hot tubs and a sauna so that he can write a novel and so that I can—what? It is unclear what I do.

You are so lucky you don't remember, my brother says as we speed away from the hospital. You were too young. (He is remembering the stroke.)

Yes, I was too young, I lie.

They sent me into intensive care with Pam! He hadn't cleared mom to go in. Pam must have been with him when they brought him. They thought she was his wife. I was the only other one let in as I was next of kin. I was fifteen. They made me go in and sit with him while he was unconscious, after the brain surgery, and it was just me and her.

Who on earth was Pam? I ask, although I know, I just didn't remember the name.

That other woman.

Ah, the switchboard girl?

Right, maybe. I don't know. I don't know what she did.

She used to call the house. Mom told me who she was. She ran the switchboard at the trucking company.

They were going to live together on the lake.

Were they?

She was friends with Feral.

Ah, that explains something, doesn't it?

Yes, he was going to quit driving trucks and give fishing tours in a boat on the lake.

Was he? Were they? That sounds so. Idyllic.

Yes, and sometimes I think, he almost made it. He almost escaped.

Yes, very nearly. Nearly escaped.

They made me go in there with him and I had to sit there.

Who made you?

Mom, and her friends. Agnes's daughter Alice, she pulled me aside and said, Don't leave him alone in there with that woman: it's your responsibility.

What does Mom say about it?

She doesn't. She says I'm wrong, I remember it wrong.

I doubt that.

I can't let go of that, being made to sit there in the ICU with that woman.

He could have escaped to the lake, I say. Isn't that crazy? How happy he would have been!

I don't tell my brother that I had talked to my father about that other woman. Much, much later, once, when I was all grown up. My father said he loved her, this other woman. He said, also, that all men really adore having two women at the same time. It makes them feel alive.

As my brother drops me off he says, I hate them all! None of them want to admit that you have done so much and that you are really a success. (I am not. I now live in a world where no one is ever successful. It no longer exists. Only my brother thinks of me as successful. He believes in another time.) They hate that most! How you have gone off and become successful. That's what they hate. The way you went off, and got away from this hellhole. They don't even believe it. They like, want to fact-check it. They can't stand it.

Who are they? I wonder. My mother's friends? My mother? Certainly not my dad, who now, as it seems, is dying in Joplin. My brother, my champion?

I have to go. I'll miss my flight. I say. Thank you, I say. Thank you for driving me. I love you, I say, though I have *never* said this to anyone in my family, and even now, I am not sure what sort of damage it does to each of us.

I go into the airport. It is Tulsa, so it is small. I don't know what happens. Perhaps I check in? I check a bag? The flight must be delayed. Significantly delayed. I have no memory. I sit and stare *into*. I feel very calm, as calm as I have ever felt, as calm as at the bottom of the aboveground pool. I sit for some time.

My husband calls my phone: Are you going to make the flight? he asks.

Yes. I think so.

Did the surgery go well?

No. I think it was bad, I say.

How so?

They cut out almost all of the colon.

But he survived the surgery. That's good.

No, it's not good. It's definitely not good.

What's next then?

I can't quite tell.

Are you alright?

I couldn't say, really, I say.

You sound checked out.

I don't remember anything after my brother dropped me off, but I think an hour has taken place, and I have a sandwich.

Dude, you don't sound well.

What if I miss my flight?

You aren't going to miss your flight; you are already there. Don't miss your flight!

What if I forget to get on?

Don't forget. I'll call you again. I'll check online to see when it leaves. I'll make sure you get on. Don't you want to go to Mont-Tremblant? There's a pool. You like pools.

Yes, I want to go. I like pools.

You can practice your French. You can eat poutine.

Yes. I like all those things.

I SIT ALONE
BY THE POOLSIDE.

Mostly, as it turns out, in Mont-Tremblant I smoke and drink wine by the poolside wearing many sweaters. I remain, well, roughly catatonic. My father is dying. Yet again, it seems. Even though it is July, in Mont-Tremblant, the weather is frigid and the swimming pool is in deep shade under many tall evergreens and slashing birch and maple trees. They drop their leaves on the surface of the pool. If I dive in, which I have done once, it almost stops my heart from the cold. Almost but not entirely. I can go into the sauna to recover and then into the hot tub. It's a cycle. The cold plunge, the hot sauna, the cold plunge, the hot tub. But mostly I sit. I am reading a novel about all these women murdered in Juárez, Mexico. Hundreds of seemingly unrelated murders of women. A town that kills women.

Why, I wonder, would anyone have thought to put a pool into this wintery ski chalet? I suppose, it is the best of all worlds.

When I am not sitting in a catatonic fashion by the side of the pool, smoking, while layered in many sweaters, and when my husband is not fever-writing a novel, we sit in the evening, in front of a fireplace, and we watch House. House is a doctor who solves the most unsolvable health things. He is also a Vicodin junkie. No one dies on House's watch.

When I leave this husband, several years later, I say, where were you when I found out my father was dying?

I was with you, he says, in Mont-Tremblant.

I only remember you writing a novel.

You remember wrong, he says. I drove you

through the mountains. I built you fires. You were so cold.

You were writing a novel and I was sitting by the pool, smoking.

You were a zombie, you were paralyzed. I couldn't get you to move. I couldn't get you to go out of the house except to drive in the car through the hills. That was all. You wouldn't leave the car. If I went to a store you would sit in the car. You were basically already a ghost. I didn't know what to do. I was with you when he died. I went with you, he says. I gave the eulogy, for Christ sake.

It's true. I can't blame him for that.

I tell someone else, Yes I don't know what happened that day in the airport, the day my brother drove me there. What happened with my brother that day in the car in that conversation? It wasn't just the botched surgery. Possibly it was this way of seeing that there was a fantasy escape route my father might have been on if he would have been lucky. There was also perhaps this indescribable pain of knowing how poorly my brother had been used, been wrecked for all time by this little tiny event. A brain event. In a tiny vessel.

I was upset, I tell a friend. I was in a confused state, in a deadened state. I could barely get on my flight, and then as the plane took off, I was crying, in not the usual way. The tears were there but as if not emotional. They weren't accompanied by, you know, sobbing or anything genuinely affective. Just like when you are really tired and your eyes water. Involuntarily.

What it sounds like, says the friend, is rage. They talk about it when someone goes on a killing spree. It's that kind of silent rage that is so encompassing it feels like you are in the eye of a storm.

walk, in his way. This was one year long, and during that year we visited him in the center where he shared a room with another sufferer, and on the door was a star with his picture in the center, a polaroid, and his head was still a patchwork, but he was smiling. Now he weighed at least enough to sink in water. He was no longer a switch, a feather, an insect. He was almost again a figure.

Then he could not walk again. The joints were collapsing inside him, the ball of his hip swirling in his socket and the leg would not behave. Now came the surgeries for the missing cartilage. First a hip, then a hip, then a shoulder, then a shoulder, and so forth. Soon he was full of aluminum. Again he must learn to walk, and so the rehab began again. Then he could stand and walk around with a shuddering, staggering gait, lurching between crutches, then between canes, then just between. Between a point and another point. Lurching home.

Back among us. Whatever we were.

THINGS CHANGE A LOT.

When he arrives home, officially, he kisses my mother on the cheek. It is the one and only time anyone sees anything like this transpire between them, and it is startling. It fills me with dread.

The arms now will not go over his head, his legs will not bend as imagined. He is covered in pink jagged scars. There is no more running or basketball or baseball with his friends. At night he sits with a tool to strengthen his hand. He squeezes the strengthening tool, while we watch Taxi.

Now things are changing, also, because I am in a different grade in a different school, and I am being treated like a real child student, at least, I go for the whole day rather than half a day, and now when I come home at the end of the day, it is not my mother waiting in the cul-de-sac, but instead it is my father, because he now stays home. My mother has returned to the secretarial desk, and not just part time. The house is being renovated. Mom-mom is going to a special home, a home where they will be able to understand her. She too is outside of language. My parents will take her portion of the house and integrate it into their lives, for betterment.

My mother visits her mother almost nightly in her new special home. I go along. In the yard of her special home, there is a mimosa tree which, when it blooms, smells of strawberries. In the hallways of her special home, the elderly sit in their wheelchairs in a state of perpetual despair. Sometimes they speak to me. Often I run from them. My mother buys mom-mom an elegant rug to cheer up the room. The rug goes missing. She buys her many fine linens, in bright colors. The linens go missing. In the home, things are transient. They are fleeting.

Now in the evening we are not simply at one with the TV. My dad and I ride bikes. Instead of anything else, there is the bike, because my father can pedal and sit, and it strengthens his legs, which are now thin white lines with long thick scars from the insertion of the new hips. So is his chest and so are his shoulders. So is his head, beneath the hair that is finally growing back, he is quilted. He is craft.

We take what my father calls the round robin. We ride down past the old airstrip, down and down past where we walked with mom-mom and Lad, our mangy grass-diseased dog, and down toward the cemetery. Through the cemetery and further still to the road that leads to the old trestle bridge, and then down a brisk long slope, on the last paved road for some time, through fields of swiftly changing wildflowers and tall grasses, in the middle of absolute nothing, until we round a bend and come slowly back into something like a residential neighborhood but a neighborhood of small farms, widely spaced on a half-paved road, and it is here that every evening, at exactly the same point, a pack of farm dogs chases me on my little bike, and though I am terrified, I ride on, at ever-increasing speeds until they give up and return to their compound. On the final turn, we come up a very steep hill, one that I can barely manage on my tiny purple one-speed. This, this difficult slope is the last stretch before home.

The speedboat is sold. The flat-bottomed boat is sold. There is no more lake, for anyone.

For my father, the language is there but not quite. He speaks, yes, but somehow not in quite the same way. He writes, but with a shaking hand, and he spells words not quite in a language of anyone's memory. He makes a shopping list and leaves it on the table for my mother. Ligt bubs? she says. Can you see this? Do you think he thinks this is how we spell light bulbs? He barely finished high school, she says. He had three different scholarships to junior colleges to play sports, and he flunked out of every one.

He does not drive trucks. That is no more. He lurches about the household. And when I get home from my new school at the end of each day, there he is, lurching about considering the yard. There are things in the yard, though not much. Has he ever noticed the yard? I think not. For so long it was the place only of the mangy dog, and the rotten walnuts dropping from the tree, mud puddles and dead grass stomped on relentlessly, and the feral child bouncing upon her swing, and the mud puddles and the inconsequential shrubbery and the chain-link fence. Here, he considers. Might there be more?

In a way, I am now the center of things. I am now the thing around which the day is organized. What luck to have such complete attention! Though now, in my new school, I am well beyond hamminess. At the new school they are teaching me a mathematical system that involves drawing little dots on all the numbers and then counting those dots. (This will ensure that I will never be able to tabulate a tip on a meal without poking spots for ten minutes. I am crippled by my learning.) They also read aloud the story of the hardships of many rabbits who, in seeking to establish a new colony, must strike out from their homeland. These rabbits are both intrepid, and gentle, and this book is accompanied by a magnificent cartoon.

But it seems, we are no longer all of us one together with the TV. My father takes himself out into the soil until very late at night, where his new burgeoning yard needs much watering. And as it begins to flourish, he is mostly at one with his garden, in a lawn chair, below the bug zapper with its hypnotic violet glow, which protects those of us with sweet flesh from the bloodsuckers.

No, now, it is only me, myself alone with the TV.

I wonder, perhaps if it is then during this period that his friend Gene kills himself in a hunting accident. And perhaps it is only the fact of the stroke that he didn't go along on this trip. I can never remember the order of things.

WHAT ELSE CHANGES.

Where did he go then that brother that was already almost not? He went further. I am told in that year while my father was in the hospital, and then in rehabilitation, in that year that I was mostly with Agnes the neighbor, my brother roamed free in the town. He did not turn up to high school where he was expected, and he did not come home, and he was not seen anywhere, but he was somewhere. Somewhere loose and away from us. He was free and alone and allowed to his thoughts.

Then when my father returned there was a cooling between them, or a cooling of a cooling, a further divide, and whatever delicate or tentative thing might have been there once was bitterly disrupted. Perhaps it was the intensive care unit. Perhaps it was the residual anger of the brain in disarray. They did not, it seemed, ever resolve this dissolution.

There is the matter of the cowboy hat and the band of turkey feathers. My father had a black felt hat, and had another made for my brother, and on both a band was sewn of wild turkey feathers which my father hunted, finally, in his slow lurch back into the woods.

He had his hat specially shaped, my brother tells me years later. We had to go to another state to get it done. I had one just like it. But this was already after the rural purge, and the feathered hat was a thing of another era, it was not the right thing for the time.

AS I LAY CATATONIC.

And such things are a delicate matter, because dislocation can end up as a dislocation of memory. Much later, when in college, when my own boyfriend from Tulsa hangs himself in front of our dog, days after our very chaotic breakup, I do not sleep so well, and so I return to my home where my father no longer lurches, but limps, less dramatically, tending his yard.

That boyfriend should in a way, not be a part of this. He was not raised in our wasteland, he was raised in a nearby wasteland, a more urban wasteland, where at the age of thirteen he was kicked out of his house, and wandered on the streets until he was adopted into a neo-Nazi compound. In those days in Oklahoma neo-Nazis and the Klan were everywhere. Perhaps this is still the case? He was kept there, anyway, this boyfriend, and was often beaten, but then escaped and lived again on the streets until his mother finally took him back, and then like a lot of teen boys from that time became a S.H.A.R.P. and kept the boots and braces, and looked for fights with neo-Nazis in the clubs, but now listened to ska, and reggae and P-funk. We met when he was twenty-two, and he was in daily AA meetings, and living with his father, an alcoholic with only half a stomach and a wretched toupee. The father lived on social security checks and bought Milwaukee's Best (Milwaukee's Beast) a six-pack at a time, and every month hocked his VCR and then got it out of hock again when he got his social security check. The boyfriend lived a block from my college campus and I could walk over from my dorms. I was eighteen. Before this, the boyfriend lived for a year in a junkyard, where he thought he had contracted TB, and before that in a storage unit where he thought he might have contracted hantavirus, and then one day he fell in a concrete drainage ditch and had to have surgery on his spleen from the damage. Who paid? I asked. No one. It went to the indigent fund, he said. That was a different time indeed.

The first time we sleep together, this boyfriend and I, I see his horrific markings: a crucified skinhead in the center of his chest, a tall boot on his bicep, a pax medallion covering over what was once a swastika on his back. He hates them all, and won't go in swimming without a shirt, for fear of scaring people. He scares himself. He looks scary without his clothes. He also walks with a limp, but since birth, because one leg is shorter than the other. Otherwise, he is nice-looking, and kind. He has learned ever so many lessons.

He wakes in the night screaming, often because he dreams he is being beaten by Nazis, or that he is beating Nazis, and I too return to having those dreams that came so often after my mom took me to see Raiders, where the Nazi in the snow raises his hand to show the burned emblem of the relic which points the way to the ark of the covenant. In my dream, when the Nazi raises his hand, in the snow, the burn on his palm is the same as the medallion on my boyfriend's back. To what, I wonder, will this point the way? I too am awake screaming, except for me this is the fantasy of a horror, whereas for my boyfriend it is the dislocated memory of a real horror. To even speak it is a delicate matter, but one that as it turns out, is not long for this world.

My boyfriend hangs himself in summer, so I go home, away from college, and stay catatonic on the sofa, mostly, day and night with my dog. Now is the time to ask questions about Gene and about the grandfather because now we are all in the same club, the club where folks tend to kill themselves, and it is not just my town, but other towns in my region that kill.

But my dad prefers not to dwell on the past. It is good to remember the dead, but it is best, perhaps, not to remember those who went there willingly. You're lucky, my dad says. How else would you ever have gotten out of that, he wonders? (Meaning that alliance with the doomed boyfriend.) You're lucky, you'll be safe now. It's not a bad thing. It's good.

How so? I lay catatonic on the sofa. Outside, my father limps in his garden. He wakes up at 4 a.m. and limps in the garden, he showers under the garden hose, he cooks his own breakfast on the griddle, and then goes to the Mullins Service Station and Rock Shop on Route 66 where he is now one of the old timers! The rock shop sold rocks in the time of the old man Mullins, and now no one ever goes into it, because who goes out of their way to buy rocks? The Mullins brothers (now in their seventies) have been doing oil changes and tire rotation for fifty years, though as the years go on, they do that sort of thing less and less, and sit around and jaw more and more with other old timers. It is a place where needling still prevails as an art form, and where there is venison chili often percolating in a crockpot, and sometimes when I have the energy to move or put on clothes, my dad takes me to the rock shop. I like the rock shop but the old timers don't like it much when my dad brings me because having a girl around makes everyone careful of their language and makes it less fun to needle.

Do you boys have any pictures of Dennis Weaver? I ask. They think, they lean upon their stools, they consider.

No, they say.

Didn't he never come in to buy some rocks? Maybe he came in to have his horse serviced? I say.

No, not to my knowledge they say, straight-faced, and they don't even know I am needling them. Perhaps I am not good enough at it on account of being a girl.

My father and I ride around on our bicycles that summer. It is one of the things he can still do that does not make all his metal joints hurt. We take the old 'round robin' but the dogs that used to chase me are now long gone, and instead there is a neat little lawn with a water feature in place of their compound.

That summer, the summer of the dead boyfriend, there is a cable channel that plays all the finest reruns: Laugh-In, The Smothers Brothers, Carol Burnett and most beloved of all beloved spy programs, The Man from U.N.C.L.E. If only, in those days I had known about The Prisoner. It was only much, much later that I learned of The Prisoner. There, in the dislocation of an island, under the striped umbrellas, in his piped suit, or perched atop a penny-farthing, the prisoner is not a number but is a free man.

THE ROOSTER'S LAMENT.

Perhaps the point is the telling. The story of my father serves as a loop such as the rooster's loop, or the barber's oscillating lament: so it's good, it's bad, how so, that's bad, no it's good, how so, and onward.

The tragedy surfacing, the possibility of the boat, the possibility of a lake, the switchboard girl, the feeling of alive, the phone calls at home, the switch bitch! The father in flight, toward freedom, delivered from the libbing women, delivered from the tantrum mouse in romper, delivered from the son in absentia, the family dissolving. The flight to the lake, the future of the lake, the possibility of another story, the stroke striking, that language lost, the brain swelling, the cortisone deployed! The brain waning, the brain in repair, the head in patchwork, in stitches, a quilt—the language returns! The body eroded, the limbs will not bend will not lurch. Begin the rehabilitation! The body reforms, is removed from the family, the body will now lurch, the father delivered. Restored to the home, the family reforming, the lake disappearing, the boat unmanned, the mistress dismissed, the cortisone still coursing, the cartilage dissolving, the joints disjointed and clanging in the limbs, the limbs do not bend, the body will not lurch, return to the infirmary, the body reopens and is restitched, the limbs now in patchwork, in quilting, the metal installed, the joints reforming, the rehabilitation begins, the walk now a lurch, the lurch now a limp, the family reforming, the family in reform.

Out of the truck, the metal carapace, into the garden, the creature lurches, his frame supported with metal, toward me, toward me, toward me in my romper, my swing, my bike, a little tantrum mouse in a tree.

ACKNOWLEDGEMENTS

I would like to gratefully acknowledge my brother, Donnie, and my belated father Joe Calvin, for being the backbone(s) of this project. I honor C.D. Wright, who pushed me to write this narrative, and whose fierceness and honesty is felt just as strongly after her passing, as in her life. She is missed and beloved.

I would also like to thank all those dedicated persons at McSweeney's for trusting and believing in this book, especially my editor Rita Bullwinkel whose brilliance and energy is incomparable. Thanks also to my agent, Allison Devereux, for her enthusiasm and savvy.

Finally, great thanks and love to Renee Gladman, Danielle Vogel, Jen Bervin, and Joanna Ruocco for their constant and continued support. To Micaela Morrisette, Andrew Bourne, and Darren Angle for their wisdom in times of loss, and to Thangam Ravindranathan and Timothy Bewes for their incomparable wit and atmospheric philosophic mentorship. And finally deep thanks to John Cayley who makes everything in the world better and more jaunty.